Abingdon's

Where the Bible Comes to Life

Preschool 6

The Whole World Celebrates Jesus

Also available from Abingdon Press:

 Abingdon's BibleZone™
Preschool 6
FUNspirational™ Kit

 Abingdon's BibleZone™
Younger Elementary 6
Teacher's Guide
Abingdon's BibleZone™
Younger Elementary 6
FUNspirational™ Kit

 Abingdon's BibleZone™
Older Elementary 6
Teacher's Guide
Abingdon's BibleZone™
Older Elementary 6
FUNspirational™ Kit

Writer/Editor: Daphna Flegal
Production Editors: Betsi Hoey Smith, Lucinda Anderson
Production and Design Manager: R. E. Osborne
Designer: Paige Easter
Cover Photo: Sid Dorris
Illustrator: Robert S. Jones

Abingdon's

Bible

Preschool 6

Where the Bible Comes to Life

THE WHOLE WORLD CELEBRATES JESUS

Abingdon Press
Nashville

> Abingdon's
> BibleZone™
> Where the Bible Comes to Life
> Preschool 6

Copyright © 1998 Abingdon Press

All rights reserved.

No part of this work, EXCEPT PATTERNS AND PAGES COVERED BY THE FOLLOWING NOTICE, may be reproduced or transmitted in any form or by an means, electronic or mechanical, including photocopying and recording, or by any information storage or retrieval system, except as may be expressly permitted by the 1976 Copyright Act or in writing from the publisher. Requests for permission should be addressed in writing to
Abingdon Press, 201 Eighth Avenue South, Nashville, TN 37203.

ISBN 0-687-093317

Unless otherwise noted, Scripture quotations are from the New Revised Standard Version of the Bible.
Copyright 1989 by the Division of Christian Education
of the National Council of Churches of Christ in the USA.
Used by permission.

Scripture quotations identified as *Good News Bible*
are from the *Good News Bible: The Bible in Today's English Version*.
Old Testament: Copyright © American Bible Society 1976, 1992;
New Testament: Copyright © American Bible Society 1966, 1971, 1976, 1992
Used by permission.

ANY PATTERN may be reproduced for use in the local church or church school
provided it is marked as **Reproducible** and the following copyright notice is included:
Permission granted to copy for local church use. © 1998 Abingdon Press.

A Cassette accompanies this resource and can be found in the FUNspirational™ Kit (0-687-09461-5). On the Cassette are all masters ⓟ Brentwood Music, Inc. and Benson Records, Inc. both divisions of the Provident Music Group, One Maryland Farms, Brentwood, TN 37207. All rights reserved. Used by permission. Unauthorized duplication prohibited.

98 99 00 01 02 03 04 05 06 07 – 10 9 8 7 6 5 4 3 2 1

MANUFACTURED IN THE UNITED STATES OF AMERICA

Table of Contents

The Whole World Celebrates Jesus

Bible Units in the Zone 6
About BibleZone™ 7
Welcome to the BibleZone™ 8
Preschoolers 9
The Angel's Message 10
Bethlehem Bound 22
Jesus Is Born! 34
Shepherds Watched 46
Simeon and Anna 58
Follow that Star! 70
Talking to God 82
A Beatitude Attitude 94
The Great Commandment 106
Forgive 118
The Least of These 130
Birds of the Field 142
The Golden Rule 154
BirthdayZone 166
Birthday Banner 167
GameZone 168
The Bible Zone 169
ChristmasZone 170
Nametags 172
All About [You] 173
BZ Bee Puppet 174
Comments from Users 175

Bible Units in the

Use these suggestions if you choose to organize the lessons in short-term units.

Nativity Stories

Bible Story	Bible Verse
The Angel's Message	I am bringing you good news of great joy for all the people. Luke 2:10
Bethlehem Bound	I am bringing you good news of great joy for all the people. Luke 2:10
Jesus Is Born!	I am bringing you good news of great joy for all the people. Luke 2:10
Shepherds Watched	I am bringing you good news of great joy for all the people. Luke 2:10
Follow that Star!	I am bringing you good news of great joy for all the people. Luke 2:10

Favorite Teachings of Jesus

Bible Story	Bible Verse
Talking to God	Teach us to pray. Luke 11:1
A Beatitude Attitude	Be happy and be glad. Matthew 5:12, *Good News Bible*
The Great Commandment	Love the Lord your God with all your heart. Matthew 22:37, *Good News Bible*
Forgive	Forgive one another. Ephesians 4:32
The Least of These	Be kind to one another. Ephesians 4:32
Birds of the Field	God cares for you. 1 Peter 5:7, adapted
The Golden Rule	Do for others what you want them do for you. Matthew 7:12, *Good News Bible*

About BibleZone

ZoneZillies:

ZoneZillies™ are game and storytelling props found in the BibleZone™ FUNspirational™ Kit. Some ZoneZillies™ are consumable and will need to be replaced. These are added for the teacher's convenience.

- Nativity prism stickers*
- inflatable bell*
- "Smile! Jesus loves you" tote
- finger puppets
- tinsel wands
- inflatable smile face*
- kazoos
- gold star confetti*
- praying hands molds
- bandanna
- jewel light* (requires two AA batteries not included)
- Cassette with music by Brentwood Kids Music

* Not recommended for children under 3.

Supplies:

- Bible
- cassette player
- two AA batteries
- construction paper
- plain paper
- mural paper or large construction paper
- glue
- glue brushes or cotton swabs
- safety scissors
- clear plastic tape
- crayons or markers
- crayons with papers removed
- gold or yellow crayons or markers
- pencils
- index cards
- shoe box
- baby doll
- paper plates
- clear tape
- masking tape
- foil cupcake liners or aluminum foil and plastic lids
- colored tissue paper
- tissues or tissue paper
- crepe paper
- newspapers
- treats (sugarless gum, small boxes of raisins, plastic toys)
- plastic bat
- paper bags
- self-sealing plastic bags
- large bowl
- stapler, staples
- cotton balls
- box lid or tray
- craft sticks, tongue depressors, or paint stirrers
- paper punch
- yarn or string
- empty cereal box

Welcome to the BibleZone

Where the Bible Comes to Life

Have fun learning about Jesus' birth and Jesus' teachings. Each lesson in this teacher guide is filled with games and activities that will make learning FUNspirational™ for you and your children. With just a few added supplies, everything you need to teach is included in the Abingdon's BibleZone™ FUNspirational™ Kit. You may want to add BZ Bee, a colorful and plush hand puppet that the children will love (see page 174). BZ Bee helps teach the Bible verse each week in the *ZoneIn™ with BZ Bee* section.

Each lesson has a ZoneIn™ box:

We know God cares about each of us.

that is repeated over and over again throughout the lesson. The ZoneIn™ states the Bible message in words your children will understand.

Use the following tips to help make your trip into the BibleZone™ a FUNspirational™ success!
- Read through each lesson. Read the Bible passages.
- Memorize the Bible verse and the ZoneIn™ statement.
- Choose activities that fit your unique group of children and your time limitations.
- Practice telling the BibleZone™ story.
- Gather the ZoneZillies™ you will use for the lesson.
- Gather supplies you will use for the lesson.
- Learn the music for the lesson from the BibleZone™ FUNspirational™ Cassette. Side 1 contains songs to celebrate the birth of Jesus. Side 2 contains songs about the teachings of Jesus.
- Arrange your room space to fit the lesson. Move tables and chairs so there is plenty of room for the children to move and sit on the floor.
- Copy the Reproducible pages for the lesson.
- Copy the HomeZone™ pages for Parents.
- Copy the nametags, All About You page (pages 172-173), and birthday page (pages 167) to use as needed with your class.

Preschoolers

Each child in your class is a one-of-a-kind child of God. Each child has his or her own name, background, family situation, and set of experiences. It is important to remember and celebrate the uniqueness of each child. Yet all of these one-of-a-kind children of God have some common needs.

- All children need love.
- All children need a sense of self-worth.
- All children need to feel a sense of accomplishment.
- All children need to have a safe place to be and express their feelings.
- All children need to be surrounded by adults who love them.
- All children need to experience the love of God.

Preschoolers (children ages 3-5 years old) also have some common characteristics.

Their Bodies
- They do not sit still for very long.
- They have lots of energy.
- They enjoy moving (running, galloping, dancing, jumping, hopping).
- They are developing fine motor skills (learning to cut with scissors, learning to handle balls, learning to tie their shoes).
- They enjoy using their senses (taste, touch, smell, hearing, seeing).

Their Minds
- They are learning more and more words.
- They enjoy music.
- They are learning to express their feelings.
- They like to laugh and be silly.
- They enjoy nonsense words.
- They are learning to identify colors, sizes, and shapes.
- They have an unclear understanding of time.
- They have wonderful imaginations.

Their Relationships
- They are beginning to interact with others as they play together.
- They are beginning to understand that other people have feelings.
- They are learning to wait for their turns.
- They can have a hard time leaving parents, especially mother.
- They want to help.
- They love to feel important.

Their Hearts
- They need to handle the Bible and see others handle it.
- They need caring adults who model Christian attitudes and behaviors.
- They need to sing, move to, and say Bible verses.
- They need to hear clear, simple stories from the Bible.
- They can express simple prayers.
- They can experience wonder and awe at God's world.
- They can share food and money and make things for others.
- They can experience belonging at church.

1 Bible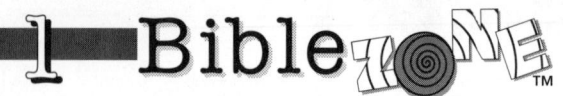

The Angel's Message

Enter the

Bible Verse
I am bringing you good news of great joy for all the people.

Luke 2:10

Bible Story
Luke 1:26-38; Matthew 1:18-25

Mary was engaged, or betrothed, to Joseph when the angel appeared to her. Betrothals in Jewish tradition were usually arranged when girls were quite young and were as legally binding as marriage. Unlike a modern engagement, a betrothal could be broken only by divorce. Both Matthew and Luke state that Jesus was conceived by the Holy Spirit, without an act by a human father. We call this the virgin birth. It is important to remember that it is the activity and power of the Holy Spirit in the birth of Jesus that is emphasized, not the lack of a human father.

Both Mary and Joseph trusted in the message they received from God. The word *angel* means "messenger." The angel's message to Mary that day was the surprising news that Mary had been chosen to be the mother of the Son of God. While she first reacted with doubt and fear, her ultimate response was one of obedience and faith. Even though she knew her life was about to be unexpectedly changed, Mary trusted God.

Mary's pregnancy was considered a sign of adultery, an offense punishable by death. When Joseph's first reaction was to divorce her quietly, he was showing care and compassion beyond the law. Like Mary, his ultimate response was to trust God.

We too are called to respond to God with the same kind of obedience and trust. As a teacher of young children you can provide a model that can influence the faith development of the children in your classroom. Preschool children are just beginning to develop a sense of trust in God. This trust is influenced by their own life experiences. Your students will come from a variety of backgrounds and family situations. All of them may not be surrounded by adults who model trust and keep promises. You can be a safe and trustworthy adult who leads your children to a sense of trust in God.

We are happy baby Jesus is born.

Scope the Zone

ZONE	TIME	SUPPLIES	ZILLIES™
Zoom Into the Zone			
Trim-a-tree	10 minutes	Reproducible 1A, crayons or markers	Nativity stickers
Top the Tree	10 minutes	Reproducibles 1A and 1B, scissors, masking tape	bandanna
BibleZone™			
Merry March	5 minutes	none	none
Sign 'n Say	5 minutes	none	none
An Angel Came	10 minutes	none	none
Bible Verse Buzz	5 minutes	Bible, BZ Bee	none
Sing!	5 minutes	cassette player	Cassette, tinsel wands
LifeZone			
Angels Fly	5 minutes	none	none
Christmas Countdown	10 minutes	Reproducible 1B, crayons or markers	none
Loop-de-loop	10 minutes	construction paper, scissors or paper cutter, glue or tape	none
Ring 'n Pray	5 minutes	none	inflatable bell

Zillies™ are found in the **BibleZone™ FUNspirational™ Kit.**

Zoom Into the Zone

Choose one or more activities to catch your children's interest.

Supplies:
Reproducible 1A, crayons or markers

Zillies™:
Nativity stickers

Trim-a-tree

Photocopy the tree picture **(Reproducible 1A)** for each child, plus one to use in class. Let the children decorate the trees with crayons or markers and **Nativity stickers**.

Say: Today our Bible story is about the time when the angel told Mary and Joseph that Mary would have a baby named Jesus. We celebrate baby Jesus' birthday on Christmas. Some people decorate Christmas trees to celebrate Jesus' birthday. People first started using Christmas trees in a country called Germany. People all over the world celebrate Jesus' birthday. People all over the world are happy baby Jesus is born.

   **We are happy baby Jesus is born.**

Supplies:
Reproducibles 1A and 1B, scissors, masking tape

Zillies™:
bandanna

Top the Tree

Mount one of the decorated Christmas trees **(Reproducible 1A)** on a door, wall, or bulletin board where the children can easily reach it. Photocopy the angel Advent calendar **(Reproducible 1B)**. Cut out the angel around the oval. Show the children the angel.

Say: Today our Bible story is about the time when the angel told Mary and Joseph that Mary would have a baby named Jesus.

Play the game like "Pin the Tail on the Donkey." Have the children come up one at a time to stand in front of the Christmas tree. Place a loop of masking tape on the back of the angel. Tie the **bandanna** around each child's head to make a blindfold. Let each child try to place the angel on the top of the Christmas tree. Replace the loop of tape as necessary.

After everyone has had a turn at the game, have the children stand in front of the Christmas tree. Sing the song printed below with the children to the tune of "London Bridge."

See the angel on the tree,
On the tree, on the tree.
See the angel on the tree.
It's Christmas time.

The angel had good news to tell.
News to tell, news to tell.
The angel had good news to tell,
It's Christmas time.

Choose one or more activities to immerse your children in the Bible story.

Merry March

Use the following movement verse to lead your children to your story area.

Follow me with a
March, march, march.
March, march, march.
March, march, march.
(March around the room.)

Follow me with a
March, march, march.
(March around the room.)
Let's have a merry Christmas.
(Shake hands in the air.)

Repeat the verse several times, substituting other words and movements for the word *march*: clap, stomp, and hop.

Supplies:
none

Zillies™:
none

Sign 'n Say

Teach the children the Bible verse, "I am bringing you good news of great joy for all the people" (Luke 2:10), using American Sign Language.

Supplies:
none

Zillies™:
none

I — hold up little finger with other fingers curled into fist. Place hand at chest.

bringing — hold both hands palms up, with one hand behind other. Move hands away from body.

you — point out with index finger.

good — touch fingers of right hand to lips. Move hand down. Place it palm up in left hand.

news — touch tips of fingers and thumb of each hand together and place at forehead. Move down and away, ending with palms up.

great — raise both hands up, with palms facing forward.

joy — pat palms of hands upward on chest several times.

all — hold left palm toward body. Use right hand to make circle out and around left hand. End with back of right hand in palm of left hand.

people — touch middle finger to thumb on both hands. Circle hands towards the center with alternating motions.

Bible Zone Story

An Angel Came

by Lorri Coates and Barbara McKone

ave the children repeat the poem and do the motions each time the poem appears in the story.

An angel came to spread the joy . . .
(Flap arms like wings.)
Mary will have a baby boy.
(Pretend to rock baby.)
A child that comes from God above,
*(Raise arms above head;
bring arms around and down at sides.)*
Born on earth to teach us love.
(Cross hands over heart.)

Long ago, God sent an angel named Gabriel to talk to a woman named Mary. *How would you feel if an angel appeared in your room?*

"Don't be afraid, Mary," said Gabriel. "You are very special. You are so special, God has chosen you to give birth to a son, named Jesus. Jesus will be called the Son of God."

An angel came to spread the joy . . .
(Flap arms like wings.)
Mary will have a baby boy.
(Pretend to rock baby.)
A child that comes from God above,
*(Raise arms above head;
bring arms around and down at sides.)*
Born on earth to teach us love.
(Cross hands over heart.)

God also sent a message to a man named Joseph. An angel appeared to Joseph in a dream. Joseph was engaged to be married to Mary. The angel told Joseph that Mary would have a son named Jesus.

An angel came to spread the joy . . .
(Flap arms like wings.)
Mary will have a baby boy.
(Pretend to rock baby.)
A child that comes from God above,
(Raise arms above head; bring arms around and down at sides.)
Born on earth to teach us love.
(Cross hands over heart.)

Let's say our poem one more time.

An angel came to spread the joy . . .
(Flap arms like wings.)
Mary will have a baby boy.
(Pretend to rock baby.)
A child that comes from God above,
*(Raise arms above head;
bring arms around and down at sides.)*
Born on earth to teach us love.
(Cross hands over heart.)

Zone In With BZ Bee

Bible Verse Buzz

 Choose a child to hold the Bible open to Luke 2:10.

Say: Today our Bible story is about the time when the angel told Mary and Joseph that Mary would have a baby named Jesus. We celebrate baby Jesus' birthday on Christmas. People all over the world celebrate the good news about Jesus' birthday. People all over the world are happy baby Jesus is born.

Say the Bible verse, "I am bringing you good news of great joy for all the people" Luke 2:10), for the children. Have the children say the Bible verse after you.

Turn your back to the children or hide your hands underneath a table or behind the **BibleZone™ FUNspirational™ Kit** lid as you place the **BZ Bee puppet** (see page 174) on your hand. Turn around or bring the puppet out where the children can see it.

Pretend to make the puppet talk. Change your voice for the puppet:

Bzzz. Bzzz. Bzzz. Hi, everybody! I'm BZ Bee. *Bzzz. Bzzz. Bzzz.* I like to taste fingers. Do you have fingers? Yum, yum, yum. Let me taste.

Go to each child. Encourage, but do not force, each child to hold up his or her fingers. Have BZ pretend to taste each child's fingers. Have BZ say things like:

Mmmm. Mmmm. You taste like honey.
Bzzz. Bzzz. You taste like strawberries.
Yumm. Yumm. You taste like blueberries.

After BZ has tasted each child's fingers, say:

Bzzz. Bzzz. Bzzz. I like to taste your fingers. They're yummy. *(Rub BZ's stomach.)*

Bzzz. Bzzz. Bzzz. I like something else even more than fingers.

I like the Bible. *Bzzz. Bzzz. Bzzz.* You heard a Bible story today. Who came to visit Mary? *(an angel; Gabriel)* What did the angel tell Mary? *(Mary would have a baby named Jesus.)* Who else did the angel tell about Mary's baby? *(Joseph)*

Bzzz. Bzzz. Bzzz. Christmas is Jesus' birthday. People all over the world are happy that baby Jesus is born.

 **We are happy baby Jesus is born.**

Bzzz. Bzzz. Bzzz. Let's say the Bible verse together.

"I am bringing you good news of great joy for all the people" (Luke 2:10).

Have the children repeat the Bible verse with BZ Bee.

Have BZ Bee say good-bye to the children. Put the puppet away.

PRESCHOOL 6

15

Bible

Choose one or more activities to immerse your children in the Bible story.

Supplies:
cassette player

Zillies™:
Cassette, tinsel wands

Sing!

Have the children move to an open area of the room. Give the children the tinsel wands. Play the song "The Virgin Mary Had A Baby Boy" from the **Cassette**. Let the children move and wave the wands as the music plays.

The Virgin Mary Had A Baby Boy

De virgin Mary had a baby boy.
De virgin Mary had a baby boy.
De virgin Mary had a baby boy.
They said that His name was Jesus.

De angels sang when de baby was born.
De angels sang when de baby was born.
De angels sang when de baby was born.
They said that His name was Jesus.

He come from de glory,
He come from de glorious kingdom.
He come from de glory.
He come from de glorious kingdom.

He come from de glory.
He come from de glorious kingdom.
He come from de glory.
He come from de glorious kingdom(mm).

Arranger: Dave Williamson
Arr. © 1992 New Spring Publishing, Inc. (ASCAP) (a div. of Brentwood-Benson Music Publishing, Inc.)
All rights reserved. Used by Permission.
(Arrangement copyright refers and applies to recorded music on audiocassette.)

From the Brentwood-Benson Music Publishing, Inc. recording *Pop Candy and the Christmastime Travelers*.

Life Zone

Choose one or more activities to bring the Bible to life.

Angels Fly

Supplies:
none

Zillies™:
none

Have the children stand in a circle.

Say: Let's play a game that is played at children's parties in a country named Germany. The game is called "Ducks Fly." When I name something that really flies, flap your arms like wings. When I name something that does not fly, keep your arms still.

Call out: Ducks fly *(flap arms)*; dogs fly *(hold arms still)*; redbirds fly *(flap arms)*; butterflies fly *(flap arms)*; bumblebees fly *(flap arms)*; houses fly *(hold arms still)*; bluebirds fly *(flap arms)*; fireflies fly *(flap arms)*; cats fly *(hold arms still)*. End the game with: angels fly *(flap arms)*.

Say: Today our Bible story is about when the angel told Mary and Joseph that Mary would have a baby named Jesus. We celebrate baby Jesus' birthday on Christmas. People all over the world celebrate Jesus' birthday. People all over the world are happy baby Jesus is born.

 We are happy baby Jesus is born.

Christmas Countdown

Supplies:
Reproducible 1B, crayons or markers

Zillies™:
none

Photocopy the Advent calendar **(Reproducible 1B)** for each child. Give each child a calendar. Let the children decorate the large angel at the top of the calendar with crayons or markers.

Say: Today our Bible story is about the time when the angel told Mary and Joseph that Mary would have a baby named Jesus. We celebrate baby Jesus' birthday on Christmas. Some people use calendars to mark the days until Christmas. These calendars come from a country called Germany. People all over the world celebrate Jesus' birthday. People all over the world are happy baby Jesus is born.

Show the children the angel and star squares at the bottoms of the calendars. Count the angel and stars with the children.

Say: You can take your calendars home and color an angel or star each day from now until Christmas.

PRESCHOOL 6

Life Zone

Choose one or more activities to bring the Bible to life.

Supplies:
construction paper, scissors or paper cutter, glue or tape

Zillies™:
none

Loop-de-loops

Cut construction paper into 2-inch strips. Show the children how to glue or tape the ends of the chains and link them together. Hang the chain in your classroom.

Say: People all over the world celebrate Jesus' birthday. Some people, like the people in a country called China, decorate with paper chains to celebrate Jesus' birthday.

Supplies:
none

Zillies™:
inflatable bell

Ring 'n Pray

Have the children stand in a line. Show the children the **inflatable bell**.

Say: People all over the world celebrate Jesus' birthday. One way many people around the world celebrate is by ringing bells. Let's pretend to ring a bell to tell people everywhere that Jesus is born.

Sing the song printed below to the tune of "Are You Sleeping?" Give the bell to the child at the beginning of the line. Have the child pretend to ring the bell once and then pass it to the next child. Continue passing the bell as the children sing. Have the child at the end of the line hold on to the bell.

> Hear the bells ring,
> Hear the bells ring.
> Ding dong ding.
> Ding dong ding.
> Telling us it's Christmas,
> Telling us it's Christmas.
> Ding dong ding.
> Ding dong ding.

Have the child at the end of the line hold up the bell.

Pray: Thank you, God, for baby Jesus. Thank you, God, for (child's name).

Have the children pass the bell back down the line, pausing long enough each time for you to pray for each child as he or she holds the bell.

Photocopy the **HomeZone**™ newsletter to send home to parents.

Home Zone For Parents

The Angel's Message

Today's Bible story centers around the angel's message to Mary and Joseph: Mary would have a baby named Jesus.

The word *angel* means "messenger." Both Mary and Joseph trusted in the message they received from God.

We too are called to respond to God with trust. Pre-school children are just beginning to develop a sense of trust in God. This trust is influenced by their own life experiences. When you model trust and keep promises for your child, you are helping your child learn to trust God.

Sign 'n Say

Say the Bible verse, "I am bringing you good news of great joy for all the people" (Luke 2:10), using American Sign Language.

We are happy baby Jesus is born.

PRESCHOOL   6   Permission granted to photocopy for local church use. © 1998 Abingdon Press.

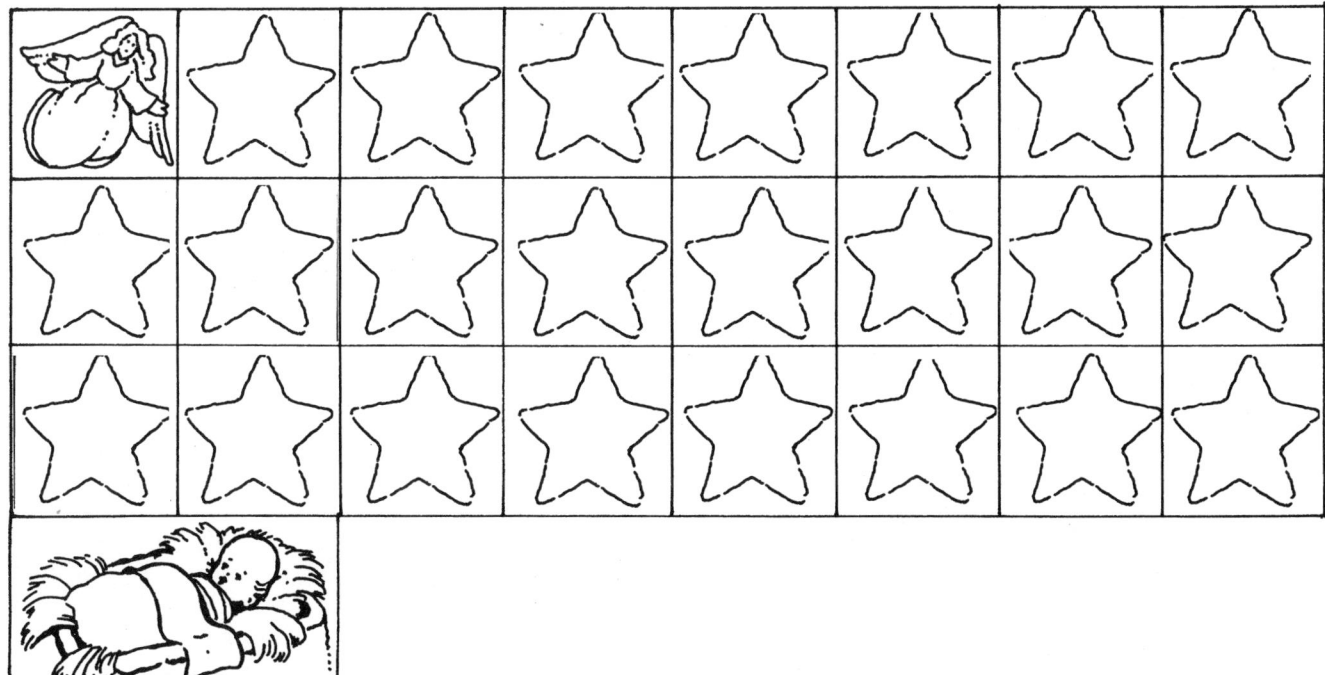

Reproducible 1B

PRESCHOOL 6

Permission granted to photocopy for local church use. © 1998 Abingdon Press.

2 Bible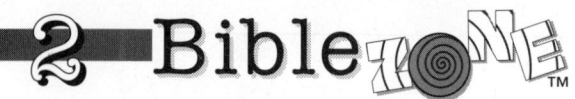

Bethlehem Bound

Enter the

Bible Verse
I am bringing you good news of great joy for all the people.

Luke 2:10

Bible Story
Luke 2:1-5

Caesar Augustus was the emperor of Rome when Mary and Joseph journeyed to Bethlehem. Caesar was the title of the office, and Augustus was the name given to him by the Roman Senate. Caesar Augustus was the grand-nephew of Julius Caesar.

Rome periodically ordered a census of the people under its rule. The government used the census as a way to raise more money for public works such as roads and aqueducts. The enrollment required that a man appear for the census in the city from which his ancestors came. Since Joseph was part of the house of David, Mary and Joseph had to travel to Bethlehem. Luke's purpose in recounting these events was more theological than historical. He wanted to show that Jesus was born in the city spoken of by the prophet Micah. ("But you, O Bethlehem of Ephrathah, who are one of the little clans of Judah, from you shall come forth for me one who is to rule in Israel, whose ancient origin is from of old, from ancient days" Micah 5:2.)

Bethlehem was on the main trade route between Jerusalem and Egypt. Caravans traveling to Egypt often stopped there. Travelers would have carried their own water, food, and other provisions because of the scarcity of water along the way. It is about ninety miles from Nazareth to Bethlehem. Mary and Joseph probably traveled by day and rested at night. While the Bible doesn't tell us how they traveled, it is likely that Mary rode on a donkey while Joseph walked by her side. It is also likely that they traveled in the company of their kinspeople, who also would be going to be counted.

Some of your children may have been on trips; others may not. Help all the children in your class experience Mary and Joseph's trip by acting it out. Do not be surprised if your children's favorite character is the donkey. Let the children begin with what interests them. They will have the opportunity to add to their understanding of the story of Jesus' birth as they grow.

Young children will not know where Bethlehem is or understand how long the trip to Bethlehem took. This lesson will help them become familiar with the name *Bethlehem* and understand that this town was special because it was the place Jesus was born.

We are happy baby Jesus is born.

Scope the Zone

ZONE	TIME	SUPPLIES	ZILLIES
Zoom Into the Zone			
Naciementos	10 minutes	Reproducible 2A, crayons or markers, shoebox, glue	none
Las Posadas	5 minutes	naciemento (Reproducible 2A) or baby doll	none
BibleZone			
Merry March	5 minutes	none	none
Sign 'n Say	5 minutes	none	none
A Trip to Bethlehem	10 minutes	none	none
Bible Verse Buzz	5 minutes	Bible, BZ Bee	none
Sing!	5 minutes	cassette player	Cassette
LifeZone			
Hop to Bethlehem	10 minutes	Reproducible 2B, masking tape	bandanna
Foil Frolics	10 minutes	foil cupcake liners or aluminum foil and plastic lids, paper punch, yarn, colored tissue paper, glue, glue brushes	none
Ring 'n Pray	5 minutes	none	inflatable bell

Zillies™ are found in the **BibleZone™ FUNspirational™ Kit**.

Zoom Into the Zone

Choose one or more activities to catch your children's interest.

Supplies:
Reproducible 2A, crayons or markers, shoebox, glue

Zillies™:
none

Naciementos

hotocopy the picture of Mary, Joseph, and baby Jesus **(Reproducible 2A)**.

Say: Today our Bible story is about the time when Mary and Joseph went to Bethlehem. Mary and Joseph packed the things they would need for the trip on a donkey. When Mary and Joseph got to Bethlehem, baby Jesus was born. We celebrate baby Jesus' birthday on Christmas. People in a country called Mexico have *naciementos*. *Naciementos* are statues of Mary, Joseph, and baby Jesus. Let's make a *naciemento*.

Let the children color the picture with crayons or markers. Fold the picture in half along the dotted line. Have the children help you glue the picture onto the outside of a shoebox.

Say: People all over the world celebrate Jesus' birthday. People all over the world are happy baby Jesus is born.

We are happy baby Jesus is born.

Supplies:
naciemento (Reproducible 2A) or baby doll

Zillies™:
none

Las Posadas

ay: One of the ways people in Mexico celebrate Jesus' birthday is by having a parade called Las Posadas. Las Posadas reminds us of Mary and Joseph's trip to Bethlehem when Jesus was born.

Choose a child to lead the parade. Give the child the naciemento **(Reproducible 2A)** to hold. If you choose not to make a naciemento, have the child hold a baby doll to represent baby Jesus. Have the other children line up behind the naciemento. Have the children walk around the room, and, if possible, outside their classroom. Have the children end their parade back into the classroom in the story area. Place the naciemento in your story area.

Say: Today our Bible story is about the time when Mary and Joseph went to Bethlehem. When Mary and Joseph got to Bethlehem, baby Jesus was born. People all over the world celebrate Jesus' birthday. People all over the world are happy baby Jesus is born.

Bible

Choose one or more activities to immerse your children in the Bible story.

Merry March

se the following movement verse to lead your children to your story area.

Follow me with a
March, march, march.
March, march, march.
March, march, march.
(March around the room.)

Follow me with a
March, march, march.
(March around the room.)
Let's have a merry Christmas.
(Shake hands in the air.)

Repeat the verse several times, substituting other words and movements for the word *march:* clap, stomp, and hop.

Supplies:
none

Zillies™:
none

Sign 'n Say

each the children the Bible verse, "I am bringing you good news of great joy for all the people" (Luke 2:10), using American Sign Language.

Supplies:
none

Zillies™:
none

I — hold up little finger with other fingers curled into fist. Place hand at chest.

bringing — hold both hands palms up, with one hand behind other. Move hands away from body.

you — point out with index finger.

good — touch fingers of right hand to lips. Move hand down. Place it palm up in left hand.

news — touch tips of fingers and thumb of each hand together and place at forehead. Move down and away, ending with palms up.

great — raise both hands up, with palms facing forward.

joy — pat palms of hands upward on chest several times.

all — hold left palm toward body. Use right hand to make circle out and around left hand. End with back of right hand in palm of left hand.

people — touch middle finger to thumb on both hands. Circle hands towards the center with alternating motions.

Bible Story

A Trip to Bethlehem

by Lorri Coates and Barbara McKone

Encourage the children to act out the preparations for a trip like the one that Mary and Joseph took to Bethlehem. Help the children think about what they would pack for a trip today, and what Mary and Joseph would have packed for their trip in Bible times.

Mary and Joseph are going to Bethlehem. Mary and Joseph lived a long time ago in Bible times. Do you think they packed their bags in their car and drove to see their relatives? No. There were no cars in Bible times. How do you think they got there? Mary and Joseph walked to Bethlehem. A donkey carried all the things they needed for the trip.

Let's all help Mary and Joseph pack for their trip to Bethlehem. Everyone take out your bag *(Pretend to put a bag on the floor and open it.)* and start packing. What do you think Mary and Joseph need for their journey? Let's put the *(name things such as clothing, blankets, and whatever the children suggested)* in the bag. *(Pretend to put things into the bag.)* Mary was about to have a baby. Mary's baby would be named Jesus. What do you think they packed for the baby? Let's put the *(name things such as blankets or soft cloths and whatever the children have suggested)* in the bag. *(Pretend to put things into the bag.)* What would you pack if you were taking a trip?

Do you think Mary and Joseph took snacks to eat? What kind of food might they have taken? Let's put the *(name things such as a bread, water, and whatever the children have suggested)* in the bag. *(Pretend to put things into the bag.)* Do you think they took food for their donkey? Let's put the grain for the donkey in the bag. *(Pretend to put grain into the bag.)*

Are you ready for a trip to Bethlehem? Is your bag all packed? OK, let's all get on our donkeys. Make sure you strap your bag on tight first! *(Pretend to strap a bag to a donkey, get on, and begin to ride.)* Let's go! *(Have the children pretend to ride their donkeys and follow you around the room. Stop.)* We've been traveling a long time. I'm hungry. Let's have something to eat. *(Pretend to get off the donkey. Open the bag and get out some food. Pretend to eat.)* The donkey is hungry too. *(Pretend to reach back into the bag to get food for the donkey. Pretend to feed the donkey.)* Now it's time to ride again. *(Pretend to get back on the donkey. Have the children pretend to ride their donkeys and follow you around the room. Stop.)*

We're here! That was a big trip for Mary and Joseph, and for us. Let's all get off our donkeys and take a rest. *(Pretend to get off a donkey and sit down.)* How do you think Mary and Joseph felt when they finally got to Bethlehem?

Although their trip was sometimes difficult, Mary and Joseph knew that God was with them, taking care of them. God takes care of us too.

In With BZ Bee

Bible Verse Buzz

Choose a child to hold the Bible open to Luke 2:10.

Say: Today our Bible story is about the time when Mary and Joseph went to Bethlehem. Baby Jesus was born in Bethlehem. We celebrate baby Jesus' birthday on Christmas. People all over the world celebrate the good news about Jesus' birthday. People all over the world are happy baby Jesus is born.

Say the Bible verse, "I am bringing you good news of great joy for all the people" Luke 2:10), for the children. Have the children say the Bible verse after you.

Turn your back to the children or hide your hands underneath a table or behind the **BibleZone™ FUNspirational™ Kit** lid as you place the **BZ Bee puppet** (see page 174) on your hand. Turn around or bring the puppet out where the children can see it.

Pretend to make the puppet talk. Change your voice for the puppet:

Bzzz. Bzzz. Bzzz. Hi, everybody! I'm BZ Bee. *Bzzz. Bzzz. Bzzz.* I like to taste fingers. Do you have fingers? Yum, yum, yum. Let me taste.

Go to each child. Encourage, but do not force, each child to hold up his or her fingers. Have BZ pretend to taste each child's fingers. Have BZ say things like:

Mmmm. Mmmm. You taste like honey. *Bzzz. Bzzz.* You taste like strawberries. *Yumm. Yumm.* You taste like blueberries.

After BZ has tasted each child's fingers, say:

Bzzz. Bzzz. Bzzz. I like to taste your fingers. They're yummy. (*Rub BZ's stomach.*)

Bzzz. Bzzz. Bzzz. I like something else even more than fingers.

I like the Bible. *Bzzz. Bzzz. Bzzz.* You heard a Bible story today. Who was in the story? (*Mary, Joseph, and a donkey*) Where were Mary and Joseph going? (*Bethlehem*)

Bzzz. Bzzz. Bzzz. Christmas is Jesus' birthday. People all over the world are happy that baby Jesus is born.

 **We are happy baby Jesus is born.**

Bzzz. Bzzz. Bzzz. Let's say the Bible verse together.

"I am bringing you good news of great joy for all the people" (Luke 2:10).

Have the children repeat the Bible verse with BZ Bee.

Have BZ Bee say good-bye to the children. Put the puppet away.

Bible

Choose one or more activities to immerse your children in the Bible story.

Supplies:
cassette player

Zillies™:
Cassette

Sing!

Have the children move to an open area of the room. Play the song "That First Christmas Night" from the **Cassette.** Each time the words *clip, clop, clippity, clop* are sung, encourage the children to move like donkeys.

That First Christmas Night

The stars were bright on that first Christmas night,
   Mary and Joseph came traveling.
For many days and from far away,
   Mary and Joseph came traveling.
      Clip, Clop, Clippity, clop;
   Mary and Joseph were traveling.
      Clip, Clop, Clippity, clop;
   Mary and Joseph were traveling.

The stars were bright on that first Christmas night,
   Mary and Joseph came into town.
They found out soon that there was no room,
   Mary and Joseph came into town.
      Clip, Clop, Clippity, clop;
   Mary and Joseph were traveling.
      Clip, Clop, Clippity, clop;
   Mary and Joseph were traveling.

The stars were bright on that first Christmas night,
   Jesus was born in a cattle stall.
Bringing joy was this heav'nly boy,
   Jesus was born in a cattle stall.
      Clip, Clop, Clippity clop;
   Jesus was born in a cattle stall.
      Clip, Clop, Clippity clop;
   Jesus was born in a cattle stall.

      Clip, Clop, Clippity clop;
   Mary and Joseph were traveling.
      Clip, Clop, Clippity clop;
   Mary and Joseph were traveling,
   Mary and Joseph were traveling.

Writers: Terry Kirkland and Stan Pethel
© 1991 New Spring Publishing, Inc. (ASCAP) (a div. of Brentwood-Benson Music Publishing, Inc.)
All rights reserved. Used by permission.

From the Brentwood-Benson Music Publishing, Inc. recording *Destination: Christmas.*

Choose one or more activities to bring the Bible to life.

Hop to Bethlehem

Photocopy and cut apart the Christmas pictures **(Reproducible 2B)**. Tape the pictures to the floor in a line. Have the children stand behind the beginning of the pictures.

Say: Today our Bible story is about when Mary and Joseph went to Bethlehem. Mary and Joseph packed on a donkey the things they would need for their trip. Let's go to Bethlehem with Mary and Joseph.

Fold the **bandanna** in half to make a triangle. Make a loose knot in the center of the triangle. This will make the bandanna easy for the children to toss. Give the first child the knotted bandanna. Have the child toss the bandanna to any picture in the line.

Say: *(Child's name)* is going to Bethlehem with Mary and Joseph. *(Child's name)* will take a *(name the item pictured on the square where the bandanna landed)* on the trip. *(Child's name)* hop to the *(name the item pictured on the square where the bandanna landed)*.

Have the child hop to the picture, pick up the bandanna, and hop back to the next child in line. Give the next child the bandanna. Continue the game until every child has had a turn.

Supplies: Reproducible 2B, masking tape

Zillies™: bandanna

Foil Frolics

Say: When Mary and Joseph got to Bethlehem, baby Jesus was born. We celebrate baby Jesus' birthday on Christmas. People all over the world celebrate Jesus' birthday. One of the ways people in Mexico celebrate Jesus' birthday is by making Christmas ornaments.

Give each child a foil cupcake liner. Have the children flatten the liners. Or wrap a plastic lid from potato chip, yogurt, or margarine containers with aluminum foil for each child.

Let the children decorate the foil liners or lids with colored tissue paper. Tear the tissue paper into small pieces. Show the children how to brush glue over the liners or lids and then place the tissue paper on glue. Let the ornaments dry.

Use a paper punch to make a hole in the top of each ornament. Tie a loop of yarn through the hole to make a hanger.

Supplies: foil cupcake liners or aluminum foil and plastic lids, paper punch, yarn, colored tissue paper, glue, glue brushes

Zillies™: none

Choose one or more activities to bring the Bible to life.

Supplies:
none

Zillies™:
inflatable bell

Ring 'n Pray

Have the children stand in a line. Show the children the **inflatable bell**.

Say: People all over the world celebrate Jesus' birthday. People all over the world are happy baby Jesus is born.

 **We are happy baby Jesus is born.**

One way many people around the world celebrate is by ringing bells. Let's pretend to ring a bell to tell people everywhere that Jesus is born.

Sing the song printed below to the tune of "Are You Sleeping." Give the bell to the child at the beginning of the line. Have the child pretend to ring the bell once and then pass it to the next child. Continue passing the bell as the children sing. Have the child at the end of the line hold on to the bell.

> Hear the bells ring,
> Hear the bells ring.
> Ding dong ding.
> Ding dong ding.
> Telling us it's Christmas,
> Telling us it's Christmas.
> Ding dong ding.
> Ding dong ding.

Have the child at the end of the line hold up the bell.

Pray: Thank you, God, for baby Jesus. Thank you, God, for *(child's name)*.

Have the children pass the bell back down the line, pausing long enough each time for you to pray for each child as he or she holds the bell.

Photocopy the **HomeZone™** newsletter to send home to parents.

Home Zone For Parents

Bethlehem Bound

Today's Bible story is about Mary and Joseph's trip to Bethlehem before baby Jesus was born. It is about ninety miles from Nazareth to Bethlehem. Mary and Joseph probably traveled by day and rested at night. It is likely that Mary rode on a donkey while Joseph walked by her side.

Young children will not know where Bethlehem is or understand how long the trip to Bethlehem took. This lesson will help them become familiar with the name *Bethlehem* and understand that this town was special because it was the place Jesus was born.

Bible Verse
I am bringing you good news of great joy for all the people. Luke 2:10

Bible Story
Luke 2:1-5

Christmas Flowers

Tell your child this make-believe story based on a Mexican folktale. If your church decorates with poinsettias at Christmastime, take your child to see the flowers. Remind your child that people all over the world are happy baby Jesus is born.

"Hurry, Rosa, hurry!" Carlos shouted. Carlos and Rosa were excited. It was Christmas Eve. Everyone in the village was going to church. The children were taking flowers to fill the manger for the Christmas festival.

"Carlos, we don't have any flowers to put in the manger," said Rosa.

"We have no money," Carlos said. "We can't buy flowers without money."

Rosa and Carlos were not so excited anymore. They felt sad because they could not buy flowers for the Christmas festival. Suddenly Rosa stopped.

"Look, Carlos," said Rosa. "Here are some green flowers growing by the road."

Carlos and Rosa picked some of the flowers and hurried to church. They were happy to have flowers. They walked to the front of the church. They placed their green flowers inside the manger.

"Look what Rosa and Carlos brought," laughed some of the children. "Their flowers are weeds!"

"Listen, Rosa," said Carlos. "The other children are laughing at our flowers." Rosa and Carlos began to cry.

Suddenly the other children stopped laughing. "Look," they cried. "The flowers are changing. The flowers are red!"

Carlos and Rosa saw an amazing sight. Where they had placed their weeds, there were big, red flowers shaped like stars.

"Our flowers are beautiful," Rosa said. Rosa and Carlos were happy again. Everyone was happy to see the beautiful red flowers.

We call the flower the poinsettia. Every year it reminds us that love is the greatest gift of all.

© 1995 Cokesbury. From NEW INVITATION: Ages 3-4 Leaflets, Winter 1995-96.

We are happy baby Jesus is born.

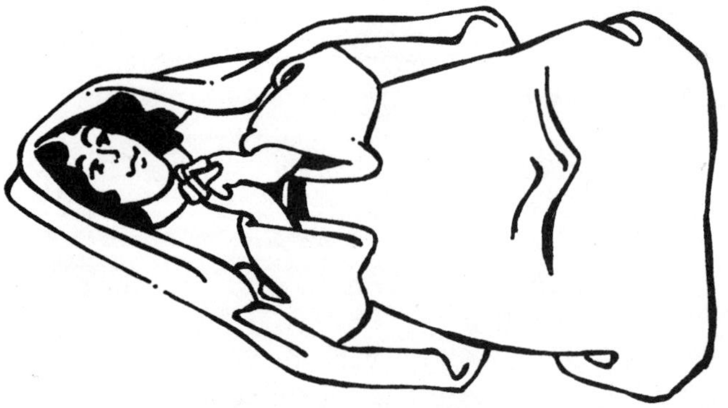

Reproducible 2A

Permission granted to photocopy for local church use. © 1998 Abingdon Press.

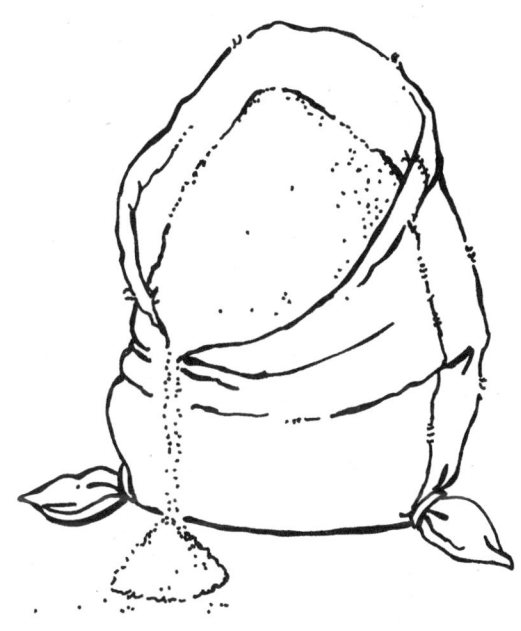
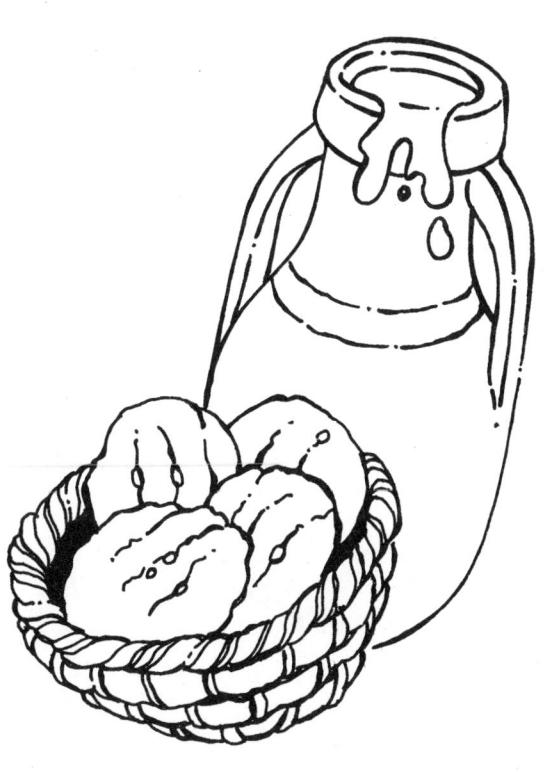
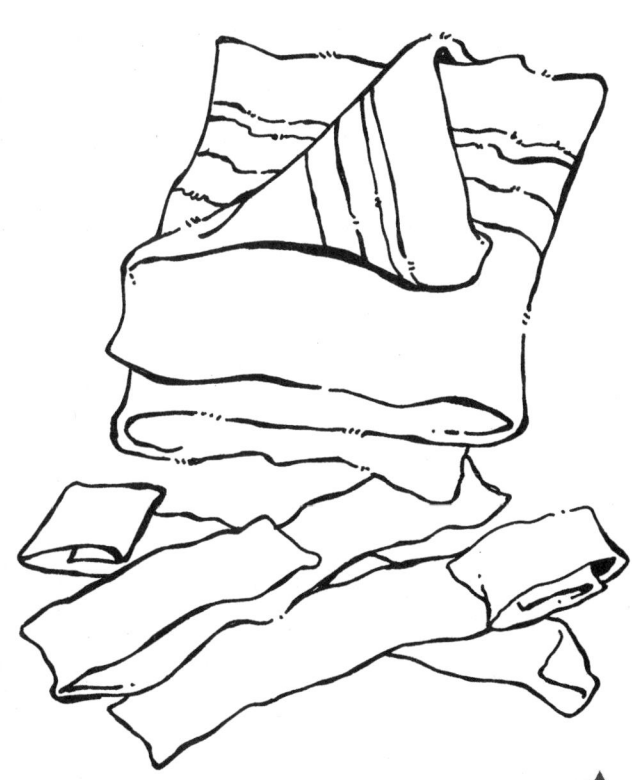

Reproducible 2B

3 Bible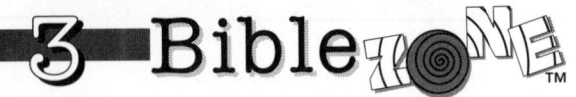

Jesus Is Born!

Enter the

Bible Verse
I am bringing you good news of great joy for all the people.

Luke 2:10

Bible Story
Luke 2:1-7

Hospitality was an important part of life in Bible times. Strangers could expect to be welcomed into people's homes as they traveled. For the time that the travelers stayed, they were considered part of the family. Because of the crowded conditions in Bethlehem, Mary and Joseph were unable to find a place to stay, either in a private home or in a guesthouse or inn.

We aren't sure exactly where Jesus was born, only that it was an area for feeding animals rather than a place of human habitation. The manger was a feeding trough for stock that might have been located under the house or a distance away in a shed or a cave. The stable or cave would have offered protection for Mary to have her baby.

After Jesus was born, Mary would have washed him and rubbed his body with salt. She knew when she set out on her journey that her son would probably be born on the trip, so she would have prepared bands of soft cloths to wrap him in. These bands of cloth would completely encircle the baby's body to keep him warm and to help his body grow straight and strong.

Few people would expect a king to be born in a stable to a poor family. We are more likely to expect a king to be born in a golden palace, with a king and queen for parents. Yet Jesus is the King of Kings. The unexpected circumstances of Jesus' birth remind us of the unexpectedness of God's action in our lives. In ways that we do not seek and in places that we do not expect, we can encounter the presence of God.

Your children are probably becoming more and more excited about Christmas Day. This season can be overstimulating for all of us, but especially for young children. This is often a time of heightened anxiety and pressure for families. Be sensitive to different family situations and to children who show that they are under pressure. Plan to use some activities that are calming during the session.

We are happy baby Jesus is born.

Scope the Zone

ZONE	TIME	SUPPLIES	ZILLIES™
Zoom Into the Zone			
No Crib for a Bed	10 minutes	Reproducible 3A, scissors, crayons or markers, tissues or tissue paper, glue	
Follow the Leader	5 minutes	none	none
BibleZone™			
Merry March	5 minutes	none	none
Sign 'n Say	5 minutes	none	none
A Happy Night!	10 minutes	mangers and baby Jesus figures (Reproducible 3A), cassette player	Cassette
Bible Verse Buzz	5 minutes	Bible, BZ Bee	none
Sing!	5 minutes	cassette player	Cassette
LifeZone			
Piñata Party	15 minutes	Reproducible 3B; construction paper, crepe paper, or colored tissue paper; glue; scissors; newspaper; string or yarn; crayons or markers; treats (sugarless gum, small boxes of raisins, small plastic toys); paper bag; self-sealing plastic bags; large bowl or paper bag; plastic bat (optional: broom handle or large dowel)	none
Ring 'n Pray	5 minutes	none	inflatable bell

Zillies™ are found in the **BibleZone™ FUNspirational™ Kit**.

PRESCHOOL 6

35

Zoom Into the Zone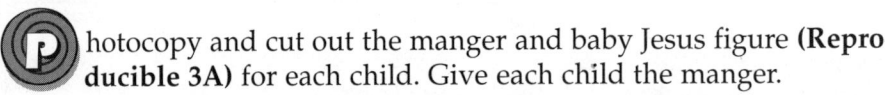

Choose one or more activities to catch your children's interest.

Supplies:
Reproducible 3A, scissors, crayons or markers, tissues or tissue paper, glue

Zillies™:
none

No Crib for a Bed

Photocopy and cut out the manger and baby Jesus figure (**Reproducible 3A**) for each child. Give each child the manger.

Say: Today our Bible story is about the time when baby Jesus was born. Baby Jesus was born in a stable, a place for animals. Mary wrapped baby Jesus in soft cloths and laid him in a manger. A manger is a place where hay was kept for the animals to eat.

Let each child decorate the manger with crayons or markers.

Give each child the baby Jesus figure. Let the children decorate the figures with crayons or markers. Tear tissue paper or tissues into small pieces. Let the children glue the pieces onto the figures to make the soft cloths for the baby Jesus figures.

Say: We celebrate Jesus' birthday on Christmas Day. People all over the world celebrate Jesus' birthday. People all over the world are happy baby Jesus is born.

 **We are happy baby Jesus is born.**

Supplies:
none

Zillies™:
none

Follow the Leader

ave the children stand in an open area of the room.

Say: People all over the world celebrate Jesus' birthday. Let's play a game the children play in a country called Vietnam. To play this game, do what I do and say what I say:

This is the way an elephant goes. (*Move like an elephant.*) Very good. Now let's pretend to be the animals that were at the stable when baby Jesus was born. This is the way a donkey goes. (*Move like a donkey.*) This is the way a sheep goes. (*Move like a sheep.*) This is the way a dove goes. (*Move like a bird.*) This is the way a cow goes. (*Move like a cow.*)

Bible

Choose one or more activities to immerse your children in the Bible story.

Merry March

 Use the following movement verse to lead your children to your story area.

Follow me with a
March, march, march
March, march, march.
March, march, march.
(March around the room.)

Follow me with a
March, march, march.
(March around the room.)
Let's have a merry Christmas.
(Shake hands in the air.)

Repeat the verse several times, substituting other words and movements for the word *march:* clap, stomp, and hop.

Supplies:
none

Zillies™:
none

Sign 'n Say

 Teach the children the Bible verse, "I am bringing you good news of great joy for all the people" (Luke 2:10), using American Sign Language.

Supplies:
none

Zillies™:
none

I — hold up little finger with other fingers curled into fist. Place hand at chest.

bringing — hold both hands palms up, with one hand behind other. Move hands away from body.

you — point out with index finger.

good — touch fingers of right hand to lips. Move hand down. Place it palm up in left hand.

news — touch tips of fingers and thumb of each hand together and place at forehead. Move down and away, ending with palms up.

great — raise both hands up with palms facing forward.

joy — pat palms of hands upward on chest several times.

all — hold left palm toward body. Use right hand to make circle out and around left hand. End with back of right hand in palm of left hand.

PRESCHOOL 6

Bible Zone Story

A Happy Night!

by Lorri Coates and Barbara McKone

Have the children bring the mangers and baby Jesus figures *(Reproducible 3A)* and sit down in a circle in the story area. Have the children place the mangers and baby figures behind them.

Imagine if you wanted to count all of the members of our Sunday school class. It would be easiest if we were all in one place, wouldn't it? Let's count out loud, and see how many friends we have here this morning. *(Count each child. Encourage the children to count with you.)* We just took a census! That's what it's called when we count all of the people from one place. A long time ago the king of the land where Mary and Joseph lived decided to take a census. The king wanted to see how many people lived in his kingdom. Mary and Joseph had to travel to Bethlehem, where Joseph's family lived, to be counted.

Mary was about to have a baby. She and Joseph looked and looked for a place to stay in Bethlehem, but there was no room. How do you think this made Mary and Joseph feel? *(Let the children respond.)*

Finally a kind innkeeper told Mary and Joseph that they could stay in his stable, the place where he kept his animals. *(Have the children place their mangers on the floor in front of them.)* Do you think that innkeeper knew what a special baby would be born in his stable? *(Let the children respond.)*

Mary and Joseph knew, and soon baby Jesus was born. *(Have the children hold their baby Jesus figures.)* Mary wrapped her baby in clean cloth to keep him warm. *(Pretend to wrap the baby figures in cloth.)* Then she laid him in a manger filled with hay. *(Place the baby figures in the mangers.)* What a beautiful baby! What a happy night!

We are so happy that baby Jesus was born! People all over the world celebrate the night when Jesus was born. One of the ways we celebrate is by singing songs that help us remember the special night when baby Jesus was born. Let's sing one now. Let's sing "Away in a Manger."

Play "Away In A Manger" from the **Cassette.** *Encourage the children to rock their baby Jesus figures as you sing the song together.*

Away In A Manger

Away in a manger, no crib for a bed,
The little Lord Jesus laid down His sweet head.
The stars in the sky looked down where he lay,
The little Lord Jesus, asleep in the hay.

The cattle are lowing, the baby awakes,
But little Lord Jesus, no crying He makes.
I love Thee, Lord Jesus! Look down from the sky,
And stay by my cradle till morning is nigh.

Be near me, Lord Jesus! I ask Thee to stay
Close by me forever, and love me, I pray.
Bless all the dear children in Thy tender care,
And fit us for heaven, to live with Thee there.

Arr. © 1987 New Spring Publishing, Inc. (ASCAP) (a div. of Brentwood-Benson Music Publishing, Inc.) All rights reserved. Used by permission. (Arrangement copyright refers and applies to recorded music on audiocassette.)

From the Brentwood Music, Inc. recording *Kids Sing Christmas*.

Zone In With BZ Bee

Bible Verse Buzz

Choose a child to hold the Bible open to Luke 2:10.

Say: Today our Bible story is about the time when baby Jesus was born in Bethlehem. We celebrate baby Jesus' birthday on Christmas. People all over the world celebrate the good news about Jesus' birthday. People all over the world are happy baby Jesus is born.

Say the Bible verse, "I am bringing you good news of great joy for all the people" Luke 2:10), for the children. Have the children say the Bible verse after you.

Turn your back to the children or hide your hands underneath a table or behind the **BibleZone™ FUNspirational™ Kit** lid as you place the **BZ Bee puppet** (see page 174) on your hand. Turn around or bring the puppet out where the children can see it.

Pretend to make the puppet talk. Change your voice for the puppet:

Bzzz. Bzzz. Bzzz. Hi, everybody! I'm BZ Bee. *Bzzz. Bzzz. Bzzz.* I like to taste fingers. Do you have fingers? Yum, yum, yum. Let me taste.

Go to each child. Encourage, but do not force, each child to hold up his or her fingers. Have BZ pretend to taste each child's fingers. Have BZ say things like:

Mmmm. Mmmm. You taste like honey.
Bzzz. Bzzz. You taste like strawberries.
Yumm. Yumm. You taste like blueberries.

After BZ has tasted each child's fingers, say:

Bzzz. Bzzz. Bzzz. I like to taste your fingers. They're yummy. *(Rub BZ's stomach.)*

Bzzz. Bzzz. Bzzz. I like something else even more than fingers.

I like the Bible. *Bzzz. Bzzz. Bzzz.* You heard a Bible story today. Who was in the story? *(Mary, Joseph, and baby Jesus)* Where was baby Jesus born? *(in a stable, in Bethlehem)*

Bzzz. Bzzz. Bzzz. Christmas is Jesus' birthday. People all over the world are happy that baby Jesus is born.

 **We are happy baby Jesus is born.**

Bzzz. Bzzz. Bzzz. Let's say the Bible verse together.

"I am bringing you good news of great joy for all the people" (Luke 2:10).

Have the children repeat the Bible verse with BZ Bee.

Have BZ Bee say good-bye to the children. Put the puppet away.

Bible

Choose one or more activities to immerse your children in the Bible story.

Supplies:
cassette player

Zillies™:
Cassette

Sing!

Have the children move to an open area of the room. Play the song "That First Christmas Night" from the **Cassette.** Each time the words *clip, clop, clippity, clop* are sung, encourage the children to move like donkeys.

That First Christmas Night

The stars were bright on that first Christmas night,
Mary and Joseph came traveling.
For many days and from far away,
Mary and Joseph came traveling.
Clip, Clop, Clippity, clop;
Mary and Joseph were traveling.
Clip, Clop, Clippity, clop;
Mary and Joseph were traveling.

The stars were bright on that first Christmas night,
Mary and Joseph came into town.
They found out soon that there was no room,
Mary and Joseph came into town.
Clip, Clop, Clippity, clop;
Mary and Joseph were traveling.
Clip, Clop, Clippity, clop;
Mary and Joseph were traveling.

The stars were bright on that first Christmas night,
Jesus was born in a cattle stall.
Bringing joy was this heav'nly boy,
Jesus was born in a cattle stall.
Clip, Clop, Clippity clop;
Jesus was born in a cattle stall.
Clip, Clop, Clippity clop;
Jesus was born in a cattle stall.

Clip, Clop, Clippity clop;
Mary and Joseph were traveling.
Clip, Clop, Clippity clop;
Mary and Joseph were traveling,
Mary and Joseph were traveling.

Writers: Terry Kirkland and Stan Pethel
© 1991 New Spring Publishing, Inc. (ASCAP) (a div. of Brentwood-Benson Music Publishing, Inc.)
All rights reserved. Used by permission.

From the Brentwood-Benson Music Publishing, Inc. recording *Destination: Christmas.*

Life

Choose one or more activities to bring the Bible to life.

Piñata Party

 hotocopy and cut out the parrot face, wings, and tail **(Reproducible 3B)**. Let the children decorate the cutouts with crayons or markers.

Say: Today our Bible story is about when baby Jesus was born. We celebrate baby Jesus' birthday on Christmas. People in a country called Mexico play a game with piñatas. A piñata is filled with treats for the children. When the piñata is broken, the treats fall down for the children to enjoy.

Let the children help you glue the parrot face, wings, and tail onto a paper bag. Have the children tear colored tissue paper, crepe paper, or construction paper into small pieces. Let the children glue the pieces all over the bag. Poke holes in the paper bag to make it easier to break. Place small boxes of raisins, sugarless gum, and other treats into the bag. Crumple newspaper and place it inside the bag to help fill the bag. Tie the bag closed with yarn or string.

Hang the piñata from the ceiling or tie the piñata to a broom handle or large dowel. If you choose to hang it from a handle or dowel, have another adult available to hold the handle or dowel.

Have the children sit in a wide circle on the floor around the piñata. Make it clear to the children that they **MUST** stay seated until the piñata is broken.

Plan for either you or another adult to break the piñata. Stand in the center of the circle with a plastic bat. Turn around several times. Encourage the children to give you directions for how to hit the piñata with the bat.

Ask: Should I step backwards? Should I swing higher? Should I step forward? Should I swing lower?

Keep your eyes open as you swing. Be aware of the children around you. If the children start to move, stop and remind them to stay seated until the piñata is broken.

When the piñata breaks, let the children move to pick up the treats. Have the children place all the treats in a large bowl or paper bag. Have the children sit around a table or in a circle on the floor. Give each child a self-sealing plastic bag. Divide the treats among the children and help them put the treats in their bags to take home.

Supplies:
Reproducible 3B; scissors; crayons or markers; glue; colored tissue paper, crepe paper, or construction paper; yarn or string; plastic bat; treats (small boxes of raisins, sugarless gum, small plastic toys), paper bag; newspaper; self-sealing plastic bags; large bowl or paper bag (optional: broom handle or large dowel)

Zillies™:
none

Life Zone

Choose one or more activities to bring the Bible to life.

Supplies:
none

Zillies™:
inflatable bell

Ring 'n Pray

ave the children stand in a line. Show the children the **inflatable bell**.

Say: People all over the world celebrate Jesus' birthday. People all over the world are happy baby Jesus is born.

 **We are happy baby Jesus is born.**

One way many people around the world celebrate is by ringing bells. Let's pretend to ring a bell to tell people everywhere that Jesus is born.

Sing the song printed below to the tune of "Are You Sleeping?" Give the bell to the child at the beginning of the line. Have the child pretend to ring the bell once and then pass it to the next child. Continue passing the bell as the children sing. Have the child at the end of the line hold on to the bell.

> Hear the bells ring,
> Hear the bells ring.
> Ding dong ding.
> Ding dong ding.
> Telling us it's Christmas,
> Telling us it's Christmas.
> Ding dong ding.
> Ding dong ding.

Have the child at the end of the line hold up the bell.

Pray: Thank you, God, for baby Jesus. Thank you, God, for *(child's name)*.

Have the children pass the bell back down the line, pausing long enough each time for you to pray for each child as he or she holds the bell.

Photocopy the **HomeZone**™ newsletter to send home to parents.

Home Zone For Parents

Bible Verse
I am bringing you good news of great joy for all the people.   Luke 2:10

Bible Story
Luke 2:1-7

A Happy Night

Today's Bible story is about the night baby Jesus was born. Mary and Joseph traveled to Bethlehem to be counted in the census. While they were there, Mary gave birth to Jesus, wrapped him in swaddling cloths, and laid him in a manger, a feeding box for animals.

After Jesus was born, Mary would have washed him and rubbed his body with salt. She then wrapped him in bands of soft cloths. These bands of cloth completely encircled the body to keep the baby warm and to help his body grow straight and strong.

Few people would expect a king to be born in a stable to a poor family. We are more likely to expect a king to be born in a golden palace, with a king and queen for parents. Yet Jesus is the King of Kings. The unexpected circumstances of Jesus' birth remind us of the unexpectedness of God's action in our lives. In ways that we do not seek and in places that we do not expect, we can encounter the presence of God.

Noel Nachos

Remind your child that people all over the world celebrate Jesus' birthday. People all over the world are happy baby Jesus is born. In a country called Mexico, people wish each other Merry Christmas in Spanish.

Feliz Navidad
(fey-LEES nah-vee-DAHD)

Enjoy a snack from Mexico. Let your child help you make cheese nachos. Purchase nachos chips or break taco shells into small pieces. Let your child sprinkle grated cheese on the chips. Melt the cheese in a microwave. Or bake in the oven at 350 degrees until the cheese is melted.

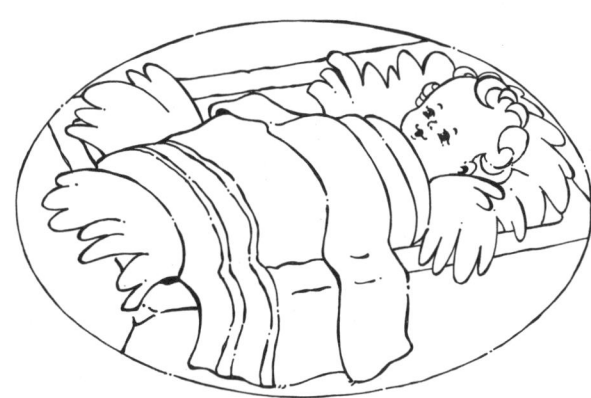

 **We are happy baby Jesus is born.**

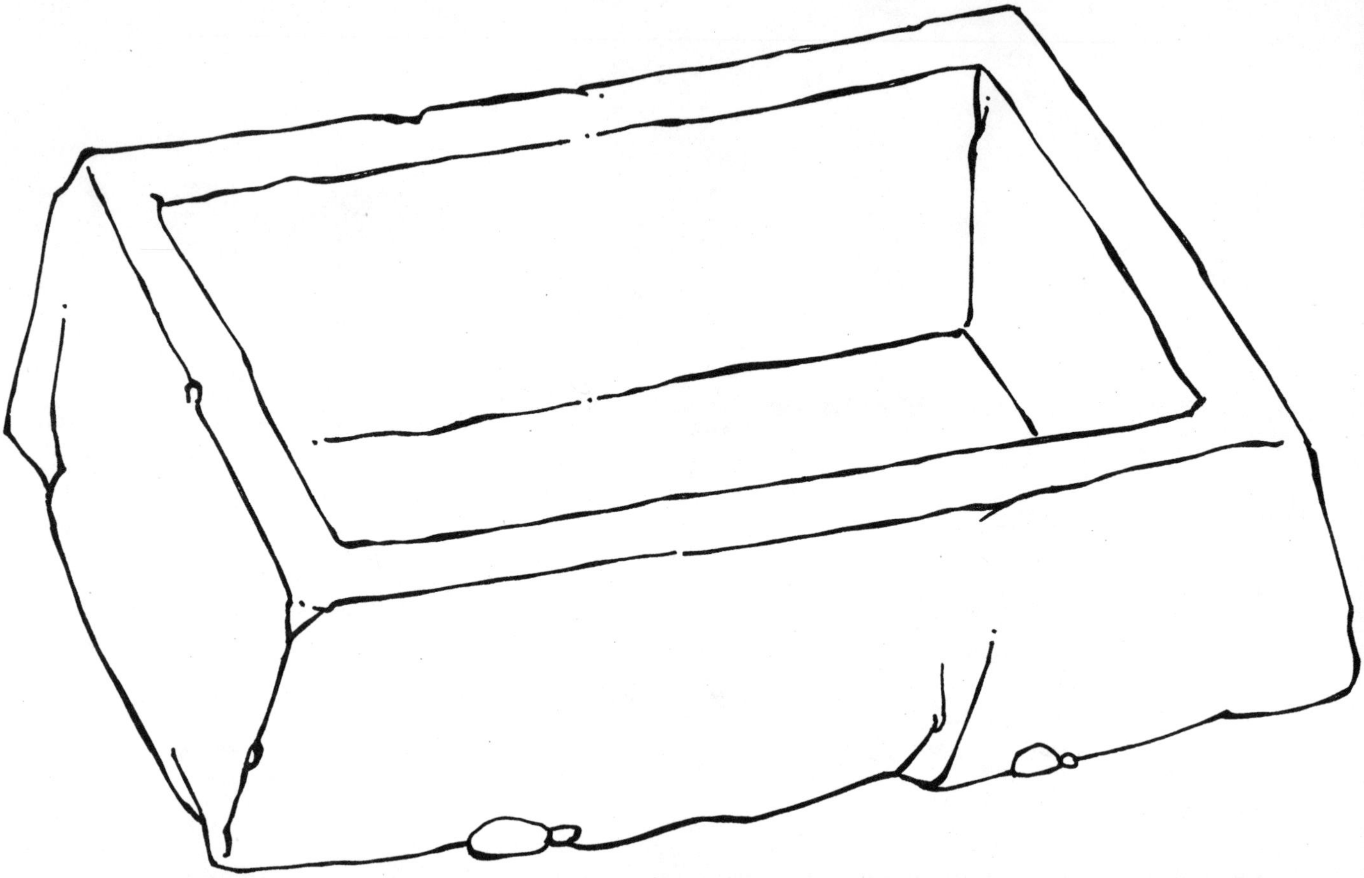

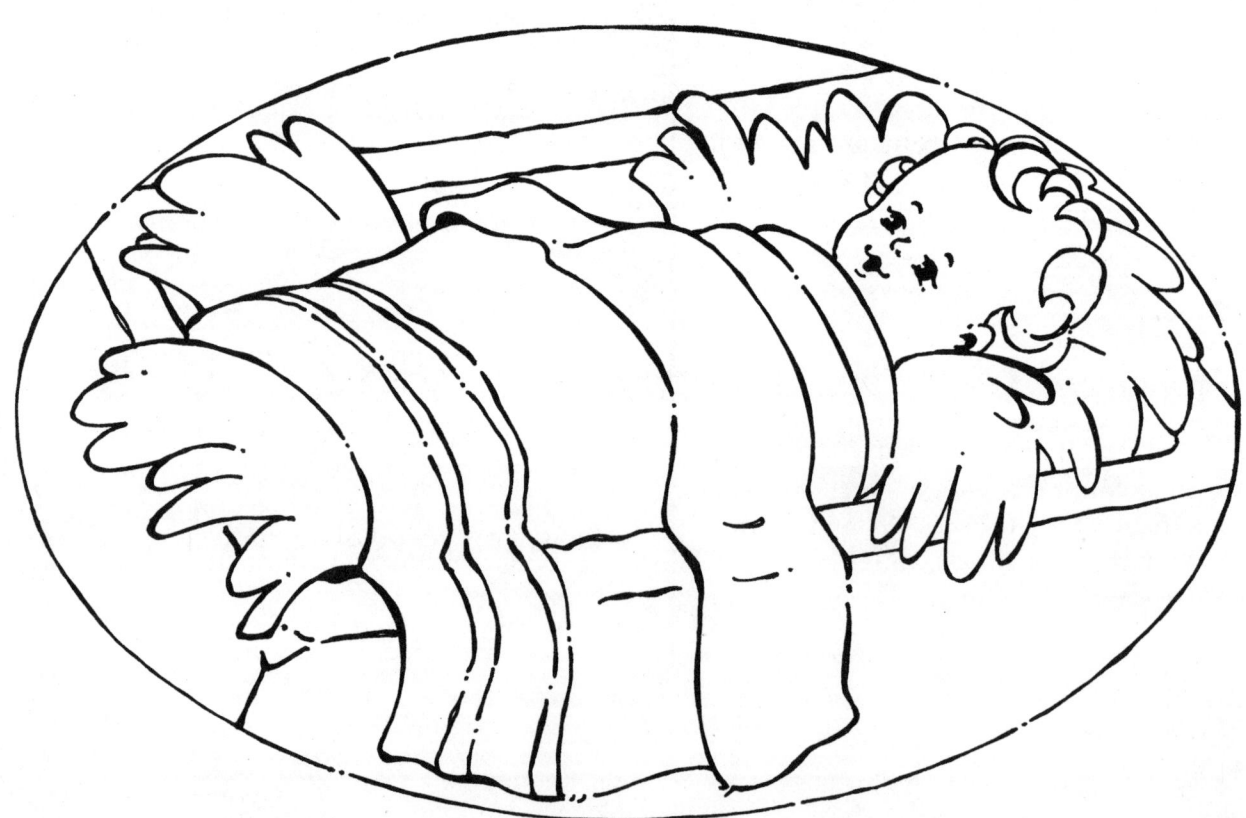

Reproducible 3A

Permission granted to photocopy for local church use. © 1998 Abingdon Press.

4 Bible

Shepherds Watched

Enter the

Bible Verse
I am bringing you good news of great joy for all the people.

Luke 2:10

Bible Story
Luke 2:8-20

The Scriptures tell us that the first to hear the good news of Jesus' birth were humble shepherds. God chose to proclaim the birth of God's Son not to kings and emperors, but rather to people in the most lowly of positions. God's greatest gift is for all people, regardless of their position in life. God's call comes to everyone.

The fields around Bethlehem do not grow lush with grass. In order for their sheep to graze, shepherds moved them about during the day. At night the shepherds drove the sheep to a common place for protection. Sometimes the sheep were kept in a sheepfold. This was either an enclosure built with a wall of rocks or a shelter built into a cave. One shepherd would lie down across the opening so that the sheep would not wander out during the night. Jesus often compared himself to a shepherd looking after sheep, and once as the door to the sheepfold.

Shepherds were simple, hardworking people. The religious leaders in the Jewish community looked down on the shepherds. Because of the very nature and difficulty of their work with the flocks, shepherds were not able to observe all the details of ceremonial law. For instance, it was impossible for them to follow all the rules and regulations of meticulous hand washing and food handling.

The shepherds were probably surprised that the Savior had been born into a peasant family and that his birth was announced first to people of lowly birth. The angel's song makes it clear — God's peace is for all.

For young children the time leading up to our celebration of the Savior's birth can be anything but peaceful. Continue to plan some quiet activities for children who might be over-stressed. Remember too that young children are still very "me" centered. Expect that your children will be more interested in what they are going to get for Christmas, rather than what they can give. Offer children opportunities to share and give to others, but do not make them feel guilty for being excited about Christmas presents. Remind your children that giving and receiving presents is one way we continue to celebrate the birth of Jesus.

ZONE IN

We are happy baby Jesus is born.

Scope the Zone

ZONE	TIME	SUPPLIES	ZILLIES
Zoom Into the Zone			
Christmas Animalitos	15 minutes	Reproducible 4A; scissors; crayons or markers; cotton balls; yarn; stapler, staples, glue or tape	none
Sheep Chase	5 minutes	none	none
BibleZone			
Merry March	5 minutes	none	none
Sign 'n Say	5 minutes	none	none
This Is the Night	10 minutes	none	none
Bible Verse Buzz	5 minutes	Bible, BZ Bee	none
Sing!	5 minutes	cassette player	Cassette, tinsel wands
LifeZone			
To Bethlehem	5 minutes	Reproducible 4B, scissors	none
Good News Gathering	5 minutes	none	none
Ring 'n Pray	5 minutes	none	inflatable bell

Zillies™ are found in the **BibleZone™ FUNspirational™ Kit.**

Zoom Into the Zone

Choose one or more activities to catch your children's interest.

Supplies:
Reproducible 4A; scissors; crayons or markers; cotton balls; yarn; stapler, staples, glue, or tape

Zillies™:
none

Christmas Animalitos

Photocopy and cut out two copies of the sheep **(Reproducible 4A)** for each child. Give each child the two copies.

Say: Today our Bible story is about the angels' message to the shepherds when baby Jesus was born. Shepherds take care of sheep. People in a country called Guatamala make cloth animals called animalitos. Let's make a sheep animalito.

Help each child place the sheep cutouts together so that the cutouts are nose to nose. Use a crayon or marker to make a dot for the eye on each sheep. Let the children use crayons or markers to decorate the side of the sheep with the eye dots.

Help each child place the two sheep pieces together so that the decorated sides face out. Staple, glue, or tape the edges of the sheep together, leaving an opening along the sheep's back. Show the children how to stuff the sheep with cotton balls. Staple, glue, or tape the opening closed. Let the children glue on strips of yarn for the sheep's tail. Place the sheep in your story area.

Say: People all over the world celebrate Jesus' birthday. People all over the world are happy baby Jesus is born.

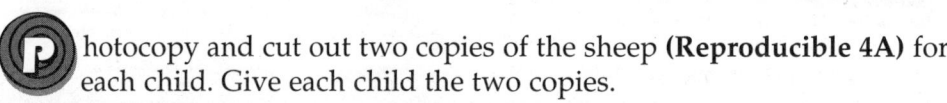

We are happy baby Jesus is born.

Supplies:
none

Zillies™:
none

Sheep Chase

Say: **Let's play a game children play in a country called Egypt. To play the game, let's pretend that we are sheep.**

Have the children move to an open area of the room and stand in a circle. Choose one child to be in the middle. This child is the wolf. Have the children shout: **"Wolf, wolf, what are you doing?"** Have the wolf answer, **"I'm sleeping."** Have the children keep shouting at the wolf. Then have the wolf shout, **"I'm chasing you!"** Have the wolf chase after the sheep. The first sheep caught is the next wolf.

Bible

Choose one or more activities to immerse your children in the Bible story.

Merry March

se the following movement verse to lead your children to your story area.

Follow me with a
March, march, march.
March, march, march.
March, march, march.
(March around the room.)

Follow me with a
March, march, march.
(March around the room.)
Let's have a merry Christmas.
(Shake hands in the air.)

Repeat the verse several times, substituting other words and movements for the word *march:* clap, stomp, and hop.

Sign 'n Say

each the children the Bible verse, "I am bringing you good news of great joy for all the people" (Luke 2:10), using American Sign Language.

Supplies:
none

Zillies™:
none

Supplies:
none

Zillies™:
none

I — hold up little finger with other fingers curled into fist. Place hand at chest.

bringing — hold both hands palms up, with one hand behind other. Move hands away from body.

you — point out with index finger.

good — touch fingers of right hand to lips. Move hand down. Place it palm up in left hand.

news — touch tips of fingers and thumb of each hand together. Place at forehead. Move down and away, ending with palms up.

great — raise both hands up, with palms facing forward.

joy — pat palms of hands upward on chest several times.

all — hold left palm toward body. Use right hand to make circle out and around left hand. End with back of right hand in palm of left hand.

people — touch middle finger to thumb on each hand. Circle hands towards center with alternating motions.

Bible Zone Story

This Is the Night

by Lorri Coates and Barbara McKone

 ave the children stand in a circle. Encourage the children to do the motions with you as you tell the story. Or have a second teacher or helper do the motions as you tell the story.

This is the night dark and still
(Bring arms up over head; then down to sides.)
And these are the shepherds asleep on the hill
(Lean head on hands as if asleep.)
Above the city that rests and waits
(Sweep arms overhead.)
For the precious Son of God.
(Pretend to rock baby.)

This is the light that glows all around
(Move arms in wide circle.)
The angels who sing with a glorious sound,
(Fold hands in prayer.)
"Good news, great joy and love abound
(Cup hands around mouth.)
For the precious Son of God."
(Pretend to rock baby.)

These are the shepherds so afraid
(Pretend to shake with fear.)
Of the mighty sound the angels made,
(Fold hands in prayer.)
"The savior is born, in a manger laid,"
(Fold arms as if holding baby.)
The precious Son of God.
(Pretend to rock baby.)

This is the song the angels sing,
(Cup hands as if singing.)
"Hallelujah to the King!
(Raise arms above head.)
Glory to God and honor bring
(Bring arms out as if holding a gift.)
To the precious Son of God!"
(Pretend to rock baby.)

This is the town where the shepherds go
(Walk in place.)
To see the child that God loves so,
(Hold hand above eyes.)
To learn for themselves what the angels know,
(Hold hands in prayer.)
The precious Son of God.
(Pretend to rock baby.)

This is the stable warm and dry,
(Create stable roof with hands.)
With Mary and Joseph standing by,
(Stand straight and still.)
Where Jesus sleeps without a cry,
(Fold arms as if holding baby.)
The precious Son of God.
(Pretend to rock baby.)

This is the hay, soft and sweet,
(Pretend to gather a bunch of hay in your arms.)
That lies around the donkey's feet,
(Move feet as if pawing ground.)
In the place where the shepherds come to meet
(Create stable roof with hands.)
The precious Son of God.
(Pretend to rock baby.)

This is the joy the shepherds feel
(Cross hands over heart.)
As before the child they humbly kneel.
(Kneel or bow.)
The love of God they know is real,
(Wrap arms around self as in hug.)
The precious Son of God.
(Pretend to rock baby.)

This is the way the shepherds ran
(Run in place.)
To share with others God's wonderful plan.
(Turn around with arms held out from sides.)
The good news they spread as fast as they can.
(Cup hands around mouth.)
Oh! This precious Son of God!
(Pretend to rock baby.)

Zone In With BZ Bee

Bible Verse Buzz

Choose a child to hold the Bible open to Luke 2:10.

Say: Today our Bible story is about the angels' message to the shepherds when baby Jesus was born. We celebrate baby Jesus' birthday on Christmas. People all over the world celebrate the good news about Jesus' birthday. People all over the world are happy baby Jesus is born.

Say the Bible verse, "I am bringing you good news of great joy for all the people" (Luke 2:10), for the children. Have the children say the Bible verse after you.

Turn your back to the children or hide your hands underneath a table or behind the **BibleZone™ FUNspirational™ Kit** lid as you place the **BZ Bee puppet** (see page 174) on your hand. Turn around or bring the puppet out where the children can see it.

Pretend to make the puppet talk. Change your voice for the puppet:

Bzzz. Bzzz. Bzzz. Hi, everybody! I'm BZ Bee. *Bzzz. Bzzz. Bzzz.* I like to taste fingers. Do you have fingers? Yum, yum, yum. Let me taste.

Go to each child. Encourage, but do not force, each child to hold up his or her fingers. Have BZ pretend to taste each child's fingers. Have BZ say things like:

Mmmm. Mmmm. You taste like honey.
Bzzz. Bzzz. You taste like strawberries.
Yumm. Yumm. You taste like blueberries.

After BZ has tasted each child's fingers, say:

Bzzz. Bzzz. Bzzz. I like to taste your fingers. They're yummy. *(Rub BZ's stomach.)*

Bzzz. Bzzz. Bzzz. I like something else even more than fingers.

I like the Bible. *Bzzz. Bzzz. Bzzz.* You heard a Bible story today. Who came to tell shepherds baby Jesus was born? *(angels)* What did the shepherds do? *(They went to see baby Jesus.)* Whom did the shepherds tell about baby Jesus? *(everyone they met)*

Bzzz. Bzzz. Bzzz. Christmas is Jesus' birthday. People all over the world are happy that baby Jesus is born.

 **We are happy baby Jesus is born.**

Bzzz. Bzzz. Bzzz. Let's say the Bible verse together.

"I am bringing you good news of great joy for all the people" (Luke 2:10).

Have the children repeat the Bible verse with BZ Bee.

Have BZ Bee say good-bye to the children. Put the puppet away.

Bible Zone

Choose one or more activities to immerse your children in the Bible story.

Supplies:
cassette player

Zillies™:
Cassette, tinsel wands

Sing!

ave the children move to an open area of the room. Give each child a tinsel wand.

Say: The shepherds were watching their sheep on the night Jesus was born. Suddenly the shepherds saw angels in the night sky. The angels told the shepherds that baby Jesus was born in Bethlehem. Let's pretend our star wands are the stars in the sky on the night baby Jesus was born. Dance and wave your stars as the music plays.

Play the song "Silent Night, Holy Night" from the **Cassette.** Let the children move and wave the wands to the music.

Silent Night, Holy Night

Silent night, holy night,
all is calm, all is bright
'round yon virgin Mother and Child.
Holy infant so tender and mild.
Sleep in heavenly peace;
Sleep in heavenly peace.

Silent night, holy night,
all is calm, all is bright
'round yon virgin Mother and Child.
Holy infant so tender and mild.
Sleep in heavenly peace;
Sleep in heavenly peace.

Arr. © 1987 New Spring Publishing, Inc. (ASCAP) (a div. of Brentwood-Benson Music Publishing, Inc.) All rights reserved. Used by Permission.
(Arrangement copyright refers and applies to recorded music on audiocassette.)

From the Brentwood Music, Inc. recording *Kids Sing Christmas.*

Choose one or more activities to bring the Bible to life.

To Bethlehem

Supplies: Reproducible 4B, scissors

Zillies™: none

hotocopy and cut apart the angel pictures **(Reproducible 4B)**.

Say: The angels told the shepherds to go to Bethlehem to see baby Jesus. Let's pretend we are the shepherds going to Bethlehem. We will move the way the angels tell us to move.

Have the children move to one side of the room. Choose a child to begin the game. Hold up the angel cards like you would hold a hand of cards. Let the child pick a card. Show the card to all the children.

Say: The angel tells us to (describe movement illustrated in the picture chosen) **to Bethlehem.**

Have all the children move to the other side as indicated by the picture. Choose another child to pick another card. Have the children move back across the room as indicated by the picture. Continue moving back and forth across the room until you have used all the pictures.

After the children move the last time, **say: The shepherds were happy baby Jesus was born. They told everyone they met the good news about baby Jesus.**

 **We are happy baby Jesus is born.**

Good News Gathering

Supplies: none

Zillies™: none

all the children to line up for the Ring 'n Pray activity *(see page 54)*. Have the children sit down on the floor.

Say: I see someone who has good news. I see someone who (describe a child).

When the children guess who you are describing, have that child stand up and repeat the Bible verse, "I am bringing you good news of great joy for all the people" (Luke 2:10). Then have the child stand in line. Continue until you have described every child.

PRESCHOOL 6

Life Zone

Choose one or more activities to bring the Bible to life.

Supplies:
none

Zillies™:
inflatable bell

Ring 'n Pray

Have the children stand in a line. Show the children the **inflatable bell**.

Say: People all over the world celebrate Jesus' birthday. People all over the world are happy baby Jesus is born.

 **We are happy baby Jesus is born.**

One way many people around the world celebrate is by ringing bells. Let's pretend to ring a bell to tell people everywhere that Jesus is born.

Sing the song printed below to the tune of "Are You Sleeping?" Give the bell to the child at the beginning of the line. Have the child pretend to ring the bell once and then pass it to the next child. Continue passing the bell as the children sing. Have the child at the end of the line hold on to the bell.

> Hear the bells ring,
> Hear the bells ring.
> Ding dong ding.
> Ding dong ding.
> Telling us it's Christmas,
> Telling us it's Christmas.
> Ding dong ding.
> Ding dong ding.

Have the child at the end of the line hold up the bell.

Pray: Thank you, God, for baby Jesus. Thank you, God, for *(child's name)*.

Have the children pass the bell back down the line, pausing long enough each time for you to pray for each child as he or she holds the bell.

Photocopy the **HomeZone**™ newsletter to send home to parents.

BibleZone™

Home Zone For Parents

Shepherds Watched

Today's Bible story tells about the shepherds who were on the hillside watching their sheep the night Jesus was born. God chose to proclaim the birth of God's Son not to kings and emperors, but rather to people in the most lowly of positions. God's greatest gift is for all people, regardless of their position in life. God's call comes to everyone.

Bible Verse
I am bringing you good news of great joy for all the people. Luke 2:10

Bible Story
Luke 2:8-20

Cinnamon Crooks

Enjoy making cinnamon bread in the shape of shepherd crooks, or staffs, with your child.

Say: At Christmas time people all over the world celebrate Jesus' birthday. People in a country called Sweden make a special kind of bread for Christmas. Our special bread helps us remember the shepherds who were watching their sheep when baby Jesus was born.

refrigerated breadstick dough
3 tablespoons sugar
1/2 teaspoon cinnamon
1/4 cup finely chopped nuts

Preheat oven to 375 degrees. Mix together sugar, cinnamon, and nuts. Unroll breadsticks. Roll the sticks into the sugar mixture. Shape the stick into a shepherd's crook and place on a greased baking sheet. Bake for fifteen to twenty minutes.

 **We are happy baby Jesus is born.**

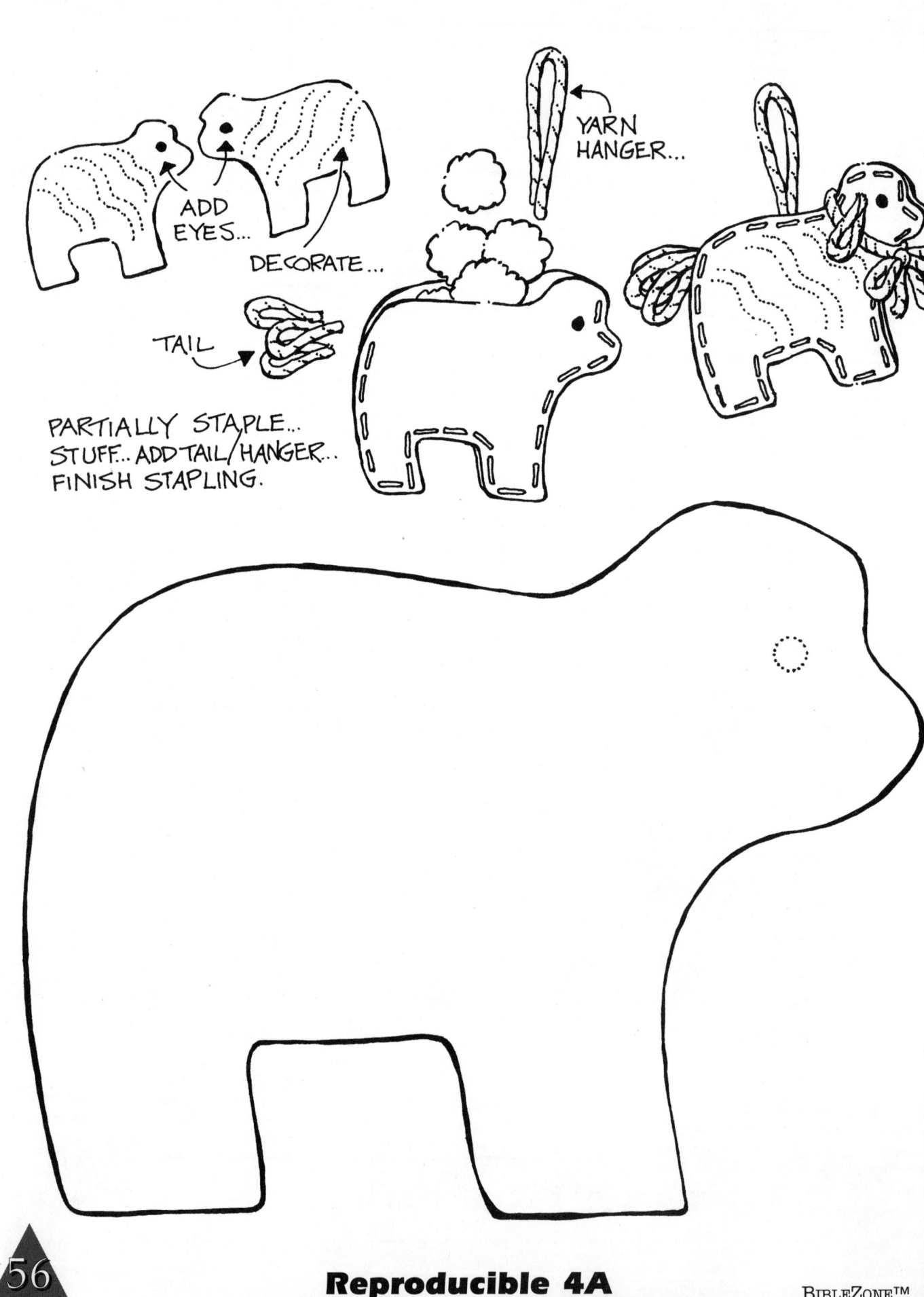

 Hop

 Crawl

 Tiptoe

 Walk Backwards

Reproducible 4B

5 BibleZone

Simeon and Anna

Enter the Zone

Bible Verse
I am bringing you good news of great joy for all the people.

Luke 2:10

Bible Story
Luke 2:22-38

Luke seems to have combined two Old Testament rituals, the ceremony of purification and the redemption of the firstborn. Forty days following the birth of her child, a woman was required to offer a sacrifice consisting of a lamb, or for a poor woman, a pair of turtledoves or two young pigeons. This was the ceremony of purification. According to Jewish custom the firstborn boy in a family belonged to the Lord and must be redeemed with a offering of five shekels. This offering was made by the father in a ceremony called the redemption of the firstborn. It is certainly possible, of course, that Mary and Joseph themselves combined the two rituals. The important thing is that they were together at the Temple—or more likely in the Temple courtyard, since both Mary and Anna were present.

Simeon, an aged prophet, had been awaiting the birth of the Messiah. When he saw the parents of Jesus performing their duties, it was clear to him that in Jesus his hopes were fulfilled. Taking the baby in his arms, he sang a song of praise and thanksgiving and then offered a special blessing to Mary.

At the same time, Anna, a prophetess who lived in the Temple, saw baby Jesus. She too began to praise God for the birth of a baby who would lead his people to salvation.

Young children can understand the excitement with which people greet the birth of a baby, and they can understand special rituals revolving around the baby that take place both in the home and at church. Talk with your children about special people in their lives who help them celebrate growing up—parents, grandparents, and other relatives, special friends, neighbors, and friends at church. Talk about growth as part of God's plan for all things. Children like to see how much they have grown, and they are likely to enjoy showing you new skills as they develop. Try to plan ways to share these evidences of growth with other important people in the children's lives.

We are happy baby Jesus is born.

Scope the Zone

ZONE	TIME	SUPPLIES	ZILLIES™
Zoom Into the Zone			
Guess Who?	5 minutes	Reproducible 5A, scissors, construction paper	none
Lantern Lights	15 minutes	Reproducible 5B, paper cutter or scissors, glue or tape, crayons or markers	none
BibleZone™			
Merry March	5 minutes	none	none
Sign 'n Say	5 minutes	none	none
A Special Gift From God	10 minutes	none	none
Bible Verse Buzz	5 minutes	BZ Bee, Bible	none
Sing!	5 minutes	cassette player, lanterns (Reproducible 5B)	Cassette
LifeZone			
Ring Around the Baby	5 minutes	Reproducible 5A	none
Praise Ways	5 minutes	none	none
Ring 'n Pray	5 minutes	none	inflatable bell

Zillies™ are found in the **BibleZone™ FUNspirational™ Kit.**

Zoom Into the Zone

Choose one or more activities to catch your children's interest.

Supplies:
Reproducible 5A, construction paper, scissors

Zillies™:
none

Guess Who?

Photocopy the baby Jesus picture **(Reproducible 5A)**. Place the baby Jesus picture on the table or rug. Cut construction paper into one-inch strips. Cover the baby Jesus picture with the strips.

As the children arrive for today's lesson, show the children the covered picture. Take away one strip of paper.

Ask: Can you tell what this picture is?

Continue to remove strips of paper one at a time until the children guess that the picture is baby Jesus.

Say: Today our Bible story is about the time Mary and Joseph went to the Temple to give thanks to God for baby Jesus. Two elderly people were at the Temple. Their names were Simeon and Anna. When Simeon and Anna saw baby Jesus, they praised God. They were very happy baby Jesus was born.

We are happy baby Jesus is born.

Supplies:
Reproducible 5B, paper cutter or scissors, glue or tape, crayons or markers

Zillies™:
none

Lantern Lights

Photocopy the lantern **(Reproducible 5B)** for each child. Use scissors or a paper cutter to cut the handle from the end of the page. Give each child a lantern and handle. Let the children decorate the lanterns and handles with crayons and markers. Show each child how to fold the lantern along the dotted line so that the candles are showing. Help each child roll the lantern and glue or tape the edges together. Glue or tape the handle across the top of each lantern.

Say: People in a country called Nigeria light lanterns on Christmas Eve. The people stay up all night waiting for Christmas morning. The lanterns give them light as they sing Christmas songs. People all over the world celebrate Jesus' birthday. People all over the world are happy baby Jesus is born.

Have the children place their lanterns in your story area.

Bible

Choose one or more activities to immerse your children in the Bible story.

Merry March

Supplies:
none

Zillies™:
none

se the following movement verse to lead your children to your story area.

> Follow me with a
> March, march, march.
> March, march, march.
> March, march, march.
> *(March around the room.)*
>
> Follow me with a
> March, march, march.
> *(March around the room.)*
> Let's have a merry Christmas.
> *(Shake hands in the air.)*

Repeat the verse several times, substituting other words and movements for the word *march:* clap, stomp, and hop.

Sign 'n Say

Supplies:
none

Zillies™:
none

each the children the Bible verse, "I am bringing you good news of great joy for all the people" (Luke 2:10), using American Sign Language.

I — hold up little finger with other fingers curled into fist. Place hand at chest.

bringing — hold both hands palms up, with one hand behind other. Move hands away from body.

you — point out with index finger.

good — touch fingers of right hand to lips. Move hand down. Place it palm up in left hand.

news — touch tips of fingers and thumb of each hand together. Place at forehead. Move down and away, ending with palms up.

great — raise both hands up, with palms facing forward.

joy — pat palms of hands upward on chest several times.

all — hold left palm toward body. Use right hand to make circle out and around left hand. End with back of right hand in palm of left hand.

people — touch middle finger to thumb on both hands. Circle hands toward center with alternating motions.

PRESCHOOL 6

Bible  Story

A Special Gift From God

by Daphna Flegal

Have the children stand in a circle. Encourage the children to do the motions with you as you tell the story. Or have a second teacher or helper do the motions as you tell the story.

Wait, wait, wait.
(Cross arms over chest.)
Simeon was waiting.
He was waiting to see a special gift from God.
(Curl hands in front of eyes to make glasses.)
Wait, wait, wait.
(Cross arms over chest.)
Simeon was waiting to see baby Jesus.
(Pretend to rock a baby.)

Wait, wait, wait.
(Cross arms over chest.)
Anna was waiting.
She was waiting to see a special gift from God.
(Curl hands in front of eyes to make glasses.)
Wait, wait, wait.
(Cross arms over chest.)
Anna was waiting to see baby Jesus.
(Pretend to rock a baby.)

Look, look, look.
(Curl hands in front of eyes to make glasses.)
See baby Jesus.
Mary and Joseph brought baby Jesus to the Temple.
(Pretend to rock a baby.)
Look, look, look.
(Curl hands in front of eyes to make glasses.)
Mary and Joseph thanked God for baby Jesus.
(Pretend to rock a baby.)

Look, look, look.
(Curl hands in front of eyes to make glasses.)
Simeon saw baby Jesus.
Baby Jesus was the special gift from God.
(Pretend to rock a baby.)

Look, look, look.
(Curl hands in front of eyes to make glasses.)
Simeon thanked God for baby Jesus.
(Pretend to rock a baby.)

Look, look, look.
(Curl hands in front of eyes to make glasses.)
Anna saw baby Jesus.
Baby Jesus was the special gift from God.
(Pretend to rock a baby.)

Look, look, look.
(Curl hands in front of eyes to make glasses.)
Anna thanked God for baby Jesus.
(Pretend to rock a baby.)

Praise, praise, praise!
(Shake hands above head.)
Simeon and Anna praised God.
They were happy baby Jesus was born.
(Pretend to rock a baby.)
Praise, praise, praise!
(Shake hands above head.)
Simeon and Anna praised God for baby Jesus.
(Pretend to rock a baby.)

Praise, praise, praise!
(Shake hands above head.)
We can praise God.
We are happy baby Jesus is born.
(Pretend to rock a baby.)
Praise, praise, praise!
(Shake hands above head.)
We can praise God for baby Jesus.
(Pretend to rock a baby.)

Zone In With BZ Bee

Bible Verse Buzz

hoose a child to hold the Bible open to Luke 2:10.

Say: Today our Bible story is about the time Mary and Joseph went to the Temple to give thanks to God for baby Jesus. Two elderly people were at the Temple. Their names were Simeon and Anna. When Simeon and Anna saw baby Jesus, they praised God. They were very happy baby Jesus was born. People all over the world are happy baby Jesus is born.

Say the Bible verse, "I am bringing you good news of great joy for all the people" Luke 2:10), for the children. Have the children say the Bible verse after you.

Turn your back to the children or hide your hands underneath a table or behind the **BibleZone™ FUNspirational™ Kit** lid as you place the **BZ Bee puppet** (see page 174) on your hand. Turn around or bring the puppet out where the children can see it.

Pretend to make the puppet talk. Change your voice for the puppet:

Bzzz. Bzzz. Bzzz. Hi, everybody! I'm BZ Bee. *Bzzz. Bzzz. Bzzz.* I like to taste fingers. Do you have fingers? Yum, yum, yum. Let me taste.

Go to each child. Encourage, but do not force, each child to hold up his or her fingers. Have BZ pretend to taste each child's fingers. Have BZ say things like:

Mmmm. Mmmm. You taste like honey.
Bzzz. Bzzz. You taste like strawberries.
Yumm. Yumm. You taste like blueberries.

After BZ has tasted each child's fingers, say:

Bzzz. Bzzz. Bzzz. I like to taste your fingers. They're yummy. (*Rub BZ's stomach.*)

Bzzz. Bzzz. Bzzz. I like something else even more than fingers.

I like the Bible. *Bzzz. Bzzz. Bzzz.* You heard a Bible story today. Who was waiting for a special gift from God? (*Simeon and Anna*) What did Simeon and Anna do when they saw baby Jesus? (*They praised God.*)

Bzzz. Bzzz. Bzzz. Simeon and Anna were happy baby Jesus was born. People all over the world are happy that baby Jesus is born.

 **We are happy baby Jesus is born.**

Bzzz. Bzzz. Bzzz. Let's say the Bible verse together.

"I am bringing you good news of great joy for all the people" (Luke 2:10).

Have the children repeat the Bible verse with BZ Bee.

Have BZ Bee say good-bye to the children. Put the puppet away.

Bible Zone

Choose one or more activities to immerse your children in the Bible story.

Supplies:
cassette player, lanterns (Reproducible 5B)

Zillies™:
Cassette

Sing!

ave the children bring their lanterns (**Reproducible 5B**) and stand in an open area of the room.

Say: Simeon and Anna waited and waited to see baby Jesus. People in a country called Nigeria stay up all night waiting for Christmas morning. They light lanterns and sing Christmas songs. People all over the world celebrate Jesus' birthday. People all over the world are happy baby Jesus is born. Let's hold our lanterns and sing a Christmas song.

Play "Sing Noel" from the **Cassette**. Encourage the children to wave their lanterns as the music plays. Tell the children that the word *noel* means Christmas.

Sing Noel
(An African Nativity)

Sing Noel, Sing Noel, Noel, Noel,
Sing Noel, Sing Noel, Noel, Noel.
Sing Noel, Sing Noel, Noel, Noel,
Sing Noel, Sing Noel, Noel, Noel.

Sing we all Noel.
Sing we all Noel.
Sing we all Noel.
Sing we all Noel.
Sing we all Noel.
Sing we all Noel.
Sing we all Noel.
Sing we all Noel.

Sing Noel, Sing Noel, Noel, Noel,
Sing Noel, Sing Noel, Noel, Noel.
Sing Noel, Sing Noel, Noel, Noel,
Sing Noel, Sing Noel, Noel, Noel.

Sing.
Sing.

Arranger: Dave Williamson
Arr. © 1992 New Spring Publishing, Inc. (ASCAP) (a div. of Brentwood-Benson Music Publishing, Inc.) All rights reserved. Used by Permission.
(Arrangement copyright refers and applies to recorded music on audiocassette.)

From the Brentwood-Benson Music Publishing, Inc. recording *Pop Candy and the Christmastime Travelers*.

Life

Choose one or more activities to bring the Bible to life.

Ring Around the Baby

Supplies: Reproducible 5A

Zillies™: none

Have the children stand in a circle. Place the picture of baby Jesus **(Reproducible 5A)** in the center of the circle.

Say: Simeon and Anna waited and waited for a special gift from God. Baby Jesus was that special gift. When Simeon and Anna saw baby Jesus, they praised God. Let's praise God for Jesus.

Sing the following words to the tune of "Ring Around the Rosie." Sing the song several times and change the word *ring* to other movement words (tiptoe, skip, hop, march).

> Ring around the baby,
> This very special baby.
> Praise God for Jesus.
> Now all fall down.

Praise Ways

Supplies: none

Zillies™: none

ave the children move to an open area of the room.

Say: People all over the world praise God for Jesus. Let's play a game like children play in a country called Kenya and in a country called the United States. Let's praise God for Jesus as we play.

Sing the following words to the tune of "This Is the Way." Lead the children in the suggested motions.

This is the way we go to the Temple,
(March in place.)
Go to the Temple, go to the Temple.
This is the way we go to the Temple,
And thank God for Jesus.
(Clap hands and turn around.)

This is the way we see the baby,
(Make glasses with hands.)
See the baby, see the baby.
This is the way we see the baby,
And thank God for Jesus.
(Clap hands and turn around.)

This is the way we hold the baby,
(Pretend to rock baby.)
Hold the baby, hold the baby.
This is the way we hold the baby,
And thank God for Jesus.
(Clap hands and turn around.)

This is the way we show our praise,
(Shake hands above head.)
Show our praise, show our praise.
This is the way we show our praise,
And thank God for Jesus.
(Clap hands and turn around.)

Choose one or more activities to bring the Bible to life.

Supplies:
none

Zillies™:
inflatable bell

Ring 'n Pray

Have the children stand in a line. Show the children the **inflatable bell**.

Say: People all over the world celebrate Jesus' birthday. People all over the world are happy baby Jesus is born.

 **We are happy baby Jesus is born.**

Say: One way many people around the world celebrate is by ringing bells. Let's pretend to ring a bell to tell people everywhere that Jesus is born.

Sing the song printed below to the tune of "Are You Sleeping?" Give the bell to the child at the beginning of the line. Have the child pretend to ring the bell once and then pass it to the next child. Continue passing the bell as the children sing. Have the child at the end of the line hold on to the bell.

> Hear the bells ring,
> Hear the bells ring.
> Ding dong ding.
> Ding dong ding.
> Telling us it's Christmas,
> Telling us it's Christmas.
> Ding dong ding.
> Ding dong ding.

Have the child at the end of the line hold up the bell.

Pray: Thank you, God, for baby Jesus. Thank you, God, for *(child's name)*.

Have the children pass the bell back down the line, pausing long enough each time for you to pray for each child as he or she holds the bell.

Photocopy the **HomeZone™** newsletter to send home to parents.

Home Zone For Parents

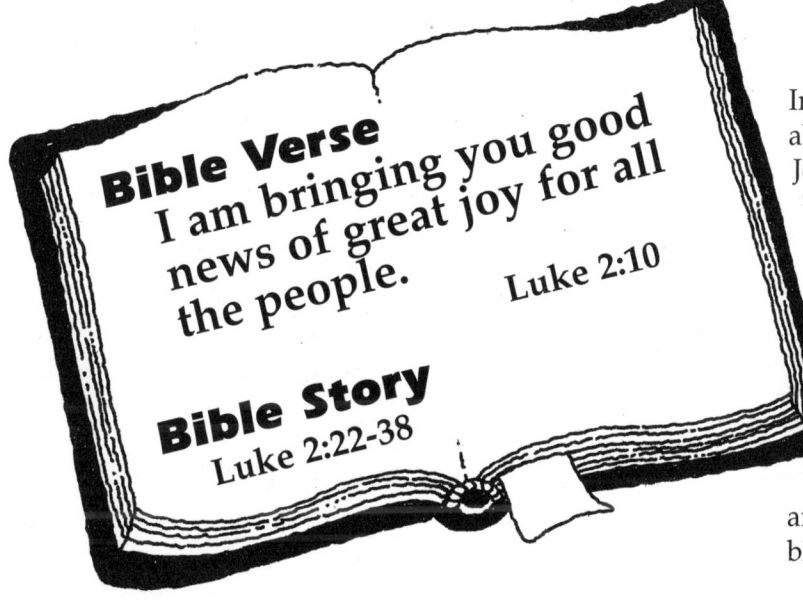

Bible Verse
I am bringing you good news of great joy for all the people. Luke 2:10

Bible Story
Luke 2:22-38

Simeon and Anna

In today's Bible story your child heard about Simeon and Anna. Mary and Joseph presented baby Jesus at the Temple when he was eight days old. Simeon, an aged prophet, had been waiting and waiting for a special gift from God, the birth of the Messiah. When he saw Mary and Joseph with Jesus, it was clear to him that Jesus was the special gift he had been waiting for. Taking the baby in his arms, he sang a song of praise and thanksgiving and then offered a blessing to Mary.

At the same time, Anna, a prophetess who lived in the Temple, saw baby Jesus. She too began to praise God for the birth of a baby who was a special gift from God.

Praise Ways

Remind your child that Simeon and Anna had waited and waited at the Temple for a special gift from God. When they saw baby Jesus, they knew that he was the special gift from God. Simeon and Anna were happy baby Jesus was born. They praised God for Jesus.

Sing the words at right to the tune of "This Is the Way" and do the motions with your child.

This is the way we go to the Temple,
(March in place.)
Go to the Temple, go to the Temple.
This is the way we go to the Temple,
And thank God for Jesus.
(Clap hands and turn around.)

This is the way we see the baby,
(Make glasses with hands.)
See the baby, see the baby.
This is the way we see the baby,
And thank God for Jesus.
(Clap hands and turn around.)

This is the way we hold the baby,
(Pretend to rock baby.)
Hold the baby, hold the baby.

This is the way we hold the baby,
And thank God for Jesus.
(Clap hands and turn around.)

This is the way we show our praise,
(Shake hands above head.)
Show our praise,
show our praise.
This is the way we
show our praise,
And thank
God for
Jesus.
*(Clap hands
and turn
around.)*

We are happy baby Jesus is born.

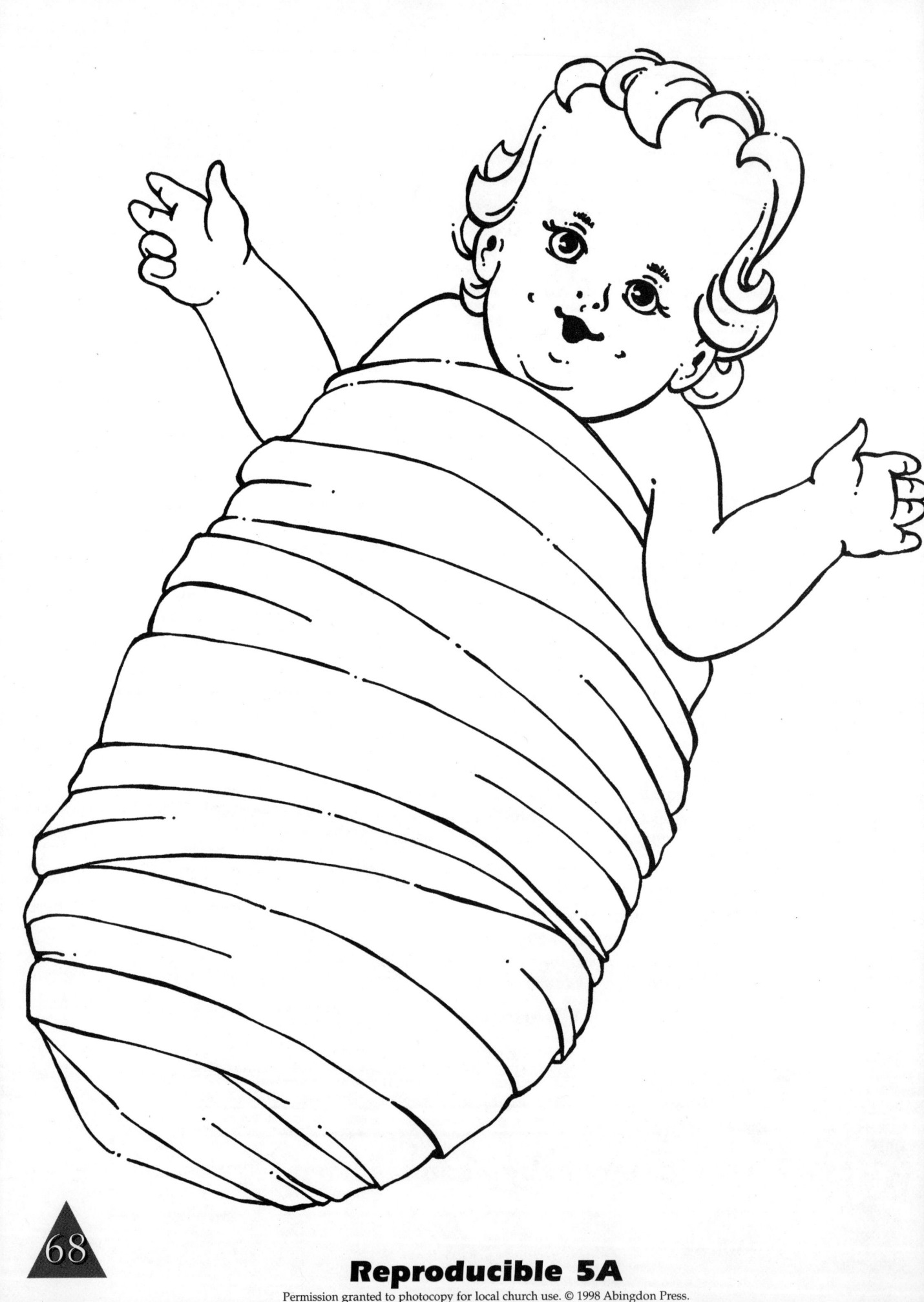

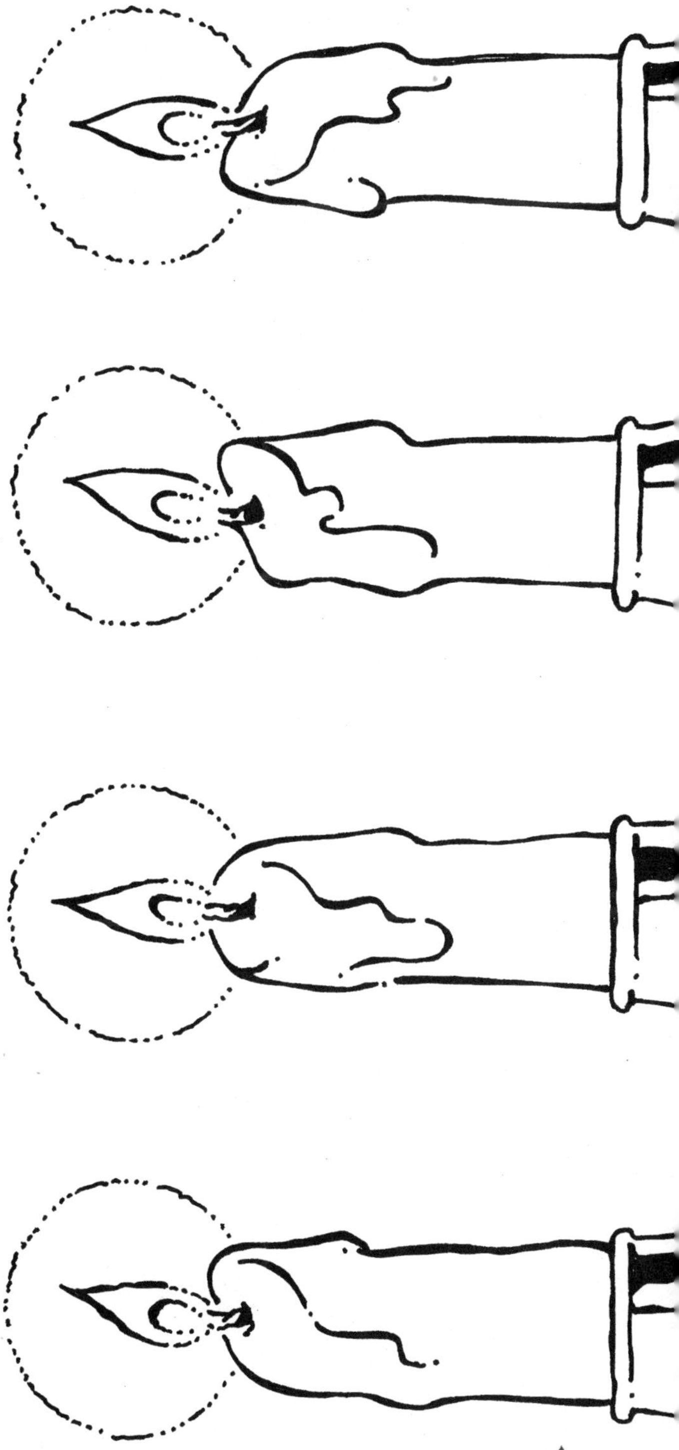

6 Bible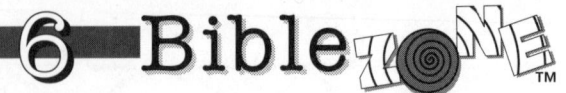

Follow that Star!

Enter the

Bible Verse
I am bringing you good news of great joy for all the people.
                                    Luke 2:10

Bible Story
Matthew 2:1-11

Matthew is the only Gospel that tells the story of wise men from the East seeing an unusual star and following it to the Christ Child. The Gospel does not say who the wise men were. Sometimes they are called by the Greek word *magi*, which refers to holy men who were skilled in science and philosophy. They were educated and influential men with the power and the means to bring gifts of luxury. Tradition holds that there were three because of the three gifts they brought.

Note that the story of the wise men refers to Jesus as "the child." Bible scholars believe that it took between two months and two years for the wise men to travel from their homes to Bethlehem.

The wise men remind us that the good news of Jesus is for all people everywhere. Sometimes, even in church, we exclude certain groups of people. Persons can be excluded because of socioeconomic differences, because of physical barriers in church buildings, or because of age. But Jesus' message of love is not just for a select group, but for everyone.

Although young children do not understand the concepts of geography, distance, and individual countries, we can help increase their awareness of the variety of cultures living within the world. We can teach our children to respect other people. We can help them enjoy and appreciate the uniqueness of various cultures.

One way we can help children learn appreciation is by inviting them to experience the foods, games, and crafts of other cultures. The Nativity stories in this BibleZone are opportunities to introduce your children to some customs from around the world. Remind your children that the birth of Jesus is celebrated by people around the world.

We are happy baby Jesus is born.

Scope the

ZONE	TIME	SUPPLIES	ZILLIES™
Zoom Into the Zone			
Star Poles	5 minutes	Reproducible 6A, scissors; crayons or markers; glue, glue brushes or cotton swabs; box lid or tray; paper plates; craft sticks, tongue depressors, or paint stirrers; tape; yarn or string	gold star confetti
Starscopes	10 minutes	Reproducible 6B, crayons or markers, tape	none
BibleZone™			
Merry March	5 minutes	none	none
Sign 'n Say	5 minutes	none	none
Twinkle, Twinkle	10 minutes	Reproducibles 6A and 6B	gold star confetti
Bible Verse Buzz	5 minutes	Bible, BZ Bee	none
Sing!	5 minutes	cassette player, star poles (Reproducible 6A, two AA batteries	Cassette, jewel light
LifeZone			
Star Catchers	10 minutes	none	none
Shining Star Circle	5 minutes	two AA batteries	jewel light
Ring 'n Pray	5 minutes	none	inflatable bell

Zillies™ are found in the **BibleZone™ FUNspirational™ Kit.**

Zoom Into the Zone

Choose one or more activities to catch your children's interest.

Supplies:
Reproducible 6A, scissors; crayons or markers; glue, glue brushes or cotton swabs; box lid or tray; paper plates; craft sticks, tongue depressors, or paint stirrers; tape; yarn or string

Zillies™:
gold star confetti

Star Poles

Photocopy and cut out the star circle **(Reproducible 6A)** for each child, plus one extra. Let the children decorate the stars with crayons or markers to make star poles. Have the children add the **gold star confetti** to their star circles. Show the children how to brush glue on their stars with brushes or cotton swabs. Place each star circle in a tray or box lid. Sprinkle the star confetti over the glue. Shake off the excess stars.

Give each child a paper plate. Have the children glue the star circle onto the center of the paper plate. Glue or tape a craft stick or tongue depressor onto the back of the plate to make a handle. Or ask paint stores to donate paint stirrers to use as handles. Show the children how to hold up the star circles by the handles.

Let the children work together to decorate one additional star circle for your story area. This star does not need a handle. Use yarn or string to hang or mount the star in your story area.

Say: Today our Bible story is about the wise men who followed the star to find the new king. People in a country called Ukraine make star poles at Christmas time. The star poles remind the people of the star that shone when Jesus was born. People all over the world celebrate Jesus' birthday. People all over the world are happy baby Jesus is born.

 **We are happy baby Jesus is born.**

Supplies:
Reproducible 6B, crayons or markers, tape

Zillies™:
none

Starscopes

Photocopy the starscope page **(Reproducible 6B)** for each child. Let the children decorate the stars with crayons or markers.

Say: Today our Bible story is about the wise men who followed the star to find the new king. Let's make telescopes so we can pretend to look at the stars.

Help each child roll the starscope page lengthwise into a tube. Tape the edges together. Show the children how to hold the starscopes up to one eye to pretend to look at the stars.

BibleZone™

Bible

Choose one or more activities to immerse your children in the Bible story.

Merry March

se the following movement verse to lead your children to your story area.

Follow me with a
March, march, march.
March, march, march.
March, march, march.
(March around the room.)

Follow me with a
March, march, march.
(March around the room.)
Let's have a merry Christmas.
(Shake hands in the air.)

Repeat the verse several times, substituting other words and movements for the word *march*: clap, stomp, and hop.

Supplies:
none

Zillies™:
none

Sign 'n Say

each the children the Bible verse, "I am bringing you good news of great joy for all the people" (Luke 2:10), using American Sign Language.

Supplies:
none

Zillies™:
none

I — hold up little finger with other fingers curled into fist. Place hand at chest.

bringing — hold both hands palms up, with one hand behind other. Move hands away from body.

you — point out with index finger.

good — touch fingers of right hand to lips. Move hand down. Place it palm up in left hand.

news — touch tips of fingers and thumb of each hand together. Place at forehead. Move down and away, ending with palms up.

great — raise both hands up, with palms facing forward.

joy — pat palms of hands upward on chest several times.

all — hold left palm toward body. Use right hand to make circle out and around left hand. End with back of right hand in palm of left hand.

people — touch middle finger to thumb on both hands. Circle hands towards the center with alternating motions.

PRESCHOOL 6

Bible  Story

Twinkle, Twinkle

by Lorri Coates and Barbara McKone

Photocopy the star circle **(Reproducible 6A)**. Decorate the star with the **gold star confetti.** *Hang or mount the star in your story area. Have the children bring their starscopes* **(Reproducible 6B)** *and stand in an area of the room opposite the star. Lead the children around the room to the star as you tell the story and do the suggested motions.*

Let's pretend that we're the wise men who followed a bright star to find a new king. Everyone, get out your starscope! *(Have the children look through their starscopes.)* Look through your starscopes at the stars. See the three stars in a line. *(Point overhead.)* Look! *(Turn your starscope so that it is facing the star in your story area.)* There's one that's brighter and larger than all of the others.

The bright star tells us that a special king has been born. We must go to find this king and bring him gifts. What shall we give him? *(Encourage the children to make suggestions.)* Put your gift in your bag and hold on to your starscope. Everyone, up on your camel. Let's go! *(Pretend to place something in a bag and then get on a camel.)* Let's sing a traveling song to make the trip go faster. *(Pretend to ride a camel as you sing the words printed below to the tune of "Twinkle, Twinkle, Little Star." Lead the children around the room.)*

> Twinkle, twinkle, shining star,
> We are wise men from afar,
> Following a star so bright,
> Looking for a king this night.
> Twinkle, twinkle, shining star,
> We are wise men from afar.

Stop and look through your starscope. *(Look through starscopes.)* See the star? It's leading us to a little town called Bethlehem. I'm getting excited, aren't you? Let's head for Bethlehem. *(Pretend to ride camels.)* Let's sing our traveling song as we go. *(Sing the words printed below to the tune of "Twinkle, Twinkle, Little Star" as you lead the children to your story area.)*

> Twinkle, twinkle, shining star,
> We are wise men from afar,
> Following a star so bright,
> Looking for a king this night.
> Twinkle, twinkle, shining star,
> We are wise men from afar.

Quick! Get out your starscopes. *(Look through starscopes.)* There it is just up that hill! A house with the star overhead! That's where we will find the new king. We're here! Tie up your camel. Open your bag and get out your gift. Everyone, knock on the door of the house. *(Pretend to knock.)* Look! The new king is Jesus! Let's lay our gifts before Jesus. *(Encourage the children to kneel and to pretend to place their gifts underneath the star.)* What a wonderful gift God has given us!

In With BZ Bee

Bible Verse Buzz

Choose a child to hold the Bible open to Luke 2:10.

Say: Today our Bible story is about the wise men who followed the star to find a special king. Jesus was the king. The wise men were very happy baby Jesus was born. People all over the world are happy baby Jesus is born.

Say the Bible verse, "I am bringing you good news of great joy for all the people" Luke 2:10), for the children. Have the children say the Bible verse after you.

Turn your back to the children or hide your hands underneath a table or behind the **BibleZone™ FUNspirational™ Kit** lid as you place the **BZ Bee puppet** (see page 174) on your hand. Turn around or bring the puppet out where the children can see it.

Pretend to make the puppet talk. Change your voice for the puppet:

Bzzz. Bzzz. Bzzz. Hi, everybody! I'm BZ Bee. *Bzzz. Bzzz. Bzzz.* I like to taste fingers. Do you have fingers? Yum, yum, yum. Let me taste.

Go to each child. Encourage, but do not force, each child to hold up his or her fingers. Have BZ pretend to taste each child's fingers. Have BZ say things like:

Mmmm. Mmmm. You taste like honey.
Bzzz. Bzzz. You taste like strawberries.
Yumm. Yumm. You taste like blueberries.

After BZ has tasted each child's fingers, say:

Bzzz. Bzzz. Bzzz. I like to taste your fingers. They're yummy. (*Rub BZ's stomach.*)

Bzzz. Bzzz. Bzzz. I like something else even more than fingers.

I like the Bible. *Bzzz. Bzzz. Bzzz.* You heard a Bible story today. Who was looking for a special king? (*the wise men*) What did the wise men follow to find the king? (*a star*) Who was the special king? (*Jesus*)

Bzzz. Bzzz. Bzzz. The wise men were happy baby Jesus was born. People all over the world are happy that baby Jesus is born.

We are happy baby Jesus is born.

Bzzz. Bzzz. Bzzz. Let's say the Bible verse together.

"I am bringing you good news of great joy for all the people" (Luke 2:10).

Have the children repeat the Bible verse with BZ Bee.

Have BZ Bee say good-bye to the children. Put the puppet away.

Bible

Choose one or more activities to immerse your children in the Bible story.

Supplies:
cassette player, star poles (Reproducible 6A), two AA batteries

Zillies™:
Cassette, jewel light

Sing!

ave the children bring their star poles and stand in an open area of the room. Place two AA batteries in the **jewel light** and turn the light on.

Say: Today our Bible story is about the wise men who followed the star to find the new king. People in a country called Ukraine make star poles at Christmas time. The star poles remind the people of the star that shone when Jesus was born. People all over the world celebrate Jesus' birthday. People all over the world are happy baby Jesus is born.

Play "Sing Noel" from the **Cassette.** Hold the jewel light in your hands. Have the children hold their star poles and make a line behind you. Hold up the jewel light and lead the children around the room as the music plays. Tell the children that the word *noel* means Christmas.

Sing Noel
(An African Nativity)

Sing Noel, Sing Noel, Noel, Noel,
Sing Noel, Sing Noel, Noel, Noel.
Sing Noel, Sing Noel, Noel, Noel,
Sing Noel, Sing Noel, Noel, Noel.

Sing we all Noel.
Sing we all Noel.
Sing we all Noel.
Sing we all Noel.
Sing we all Noel.
Sing we all Noel.
Sing we all Noel.
Sing we all Noel.

Sing Noel, Sing Noel, Noel, Noel,
Sing Noel, Sing Noel, Noel, Noel.
Sing Noel, Sing Noel, Noel, Noel,
Sing Noel, Sing Noel, Noel, Noel.

Sing.
Sing.

Arranger: Dave Williamson
Arr. © 1992 New Spring Publishing, Inc. (ASCAP) (a div. of Brentwood-Benson Music Publishing, Inc.) All rights reserved. Used by Permission.
(Arrangement copyright refers and applies to recorded music on audiocassette.)

From the Brentwood-Benson Music Publishing, Inc. recording *Pop Candy and the Christmastime Travelers*.

Choose one or more activities to bring the Bible to life.

Star Catchers

Supplies: none

Zillies™: none

Have the children move to an open area of the room.

Say: In our Bible story today the wise men followed a bright star to find Jesus. Let's play a game that children in a country called Gabon play. In this game the children pretend to be stars and star catchers. I will be the star catcher, and all of you will be the stars.

Have all the stars move to one side of the room while you stand in the middle of the room.

Say: Star light, star bright, how many stars are out tonight?

Have the stars shout: "More than you can catch!"

Then have the stars run to the opposite side of the room. Try to tag the stars as they run. Play the game several times and let the children take turns being the star catcher.

Say: The star game can remind us of the star that shone when Jesus was born. People all over the world celebrate Jesus' birthday. People all over the world are happy baby Jesus is born.

Shining Star Circle

Supplies: two AA batteries

Zillies™: jewel light

Have the children sit on the floor in a circle. Sing the song printed below to the tune of "Twinkle, Twinkle, Little Star."

> Twinkle, twinkle, shining star,
> We are wise men from afar,
> Following a star so bright,
> Looking for a king this night.
> Twinkle, twinkle, shining star,
> We are wise men from afar.

As you sing the song, pass the **jewel light** around the circle. Stop singing at any point in the song. Have the child holding the jewel light when you stopped singing stand up and say the Bible verse, "I am bringing you good news of great joy for all the people" (Luke 2:10). Continue the game until each child has been caught with the jewel light and has said the Bible verse.

Life

Choose one or more activities to bring the Bible to life.

Supplies:
none

Zillies™:
inflatable bell

Ring 'n Pray

Have the children stand in a line. Show the children the **inflatable bell**.

Say: People all over the world celebrate Jesus' birthday. People all over the world are happy baby Jesus is born.

 **We are happy baby Jesus is born.**

One way many people around the world celebrate is by ringing bells. Let's pretend to ring a bell to tell people everywhere that Jesus is born.

Sing the song printed below to the tune of "Are You Sleeping?" Give the bell to the child at the beginning of the line. Have the child pretend to ring the bell once and then pass it to the next child. Continue passing the bell as the children sing. Have the child at the end of the line hold on to the bell.

> Hear the bells ring,
> Hear the bells ring.
> Ding dong ding.
> Ding dong ding.
> Telling us it's Christmas,
> Telling us it's Christmas.
> Ding dong ding.
> Ding dong ding.

Have the child at the end of the line hold up the bell.

Pray: Thank you, God, for baby Jesus. Thank you, God, for *(child's name)*.

Have the children pass the bell back down the line, pausing long enough each time for you to pray for each child as he or she holds the bell.

Photocopy the **HomeZone™** newsletter to send home to parents.

Home Zone For Parents

Follow That Star!

Today your child heard the Bible story of the wise men following the star to the Christ Child. We do not know who the wise men were. Sometimes they are called by the Greek word *magi,* which refers to holy men who were skilled in science and philosophy. They were educated and influential men with the power and the means to bring gifts of luxury. Tradition holds that there were three of them because of the three gifts they brought.

The story of the wise men refers to Jesus as "the child." Bible scholars believe that it took between two months and two years for the wise men to travel from their homes to Bethlehem.

The wise men remind us that the good news of Jesus is for all people everywhere. Remind your child that the birth of Jesus is celebrated by people around the world.

Bible Verse
I am bringing you good news of great joy for all the people. Luke 2:10

Bible Story
Matthew 2:1-11

King's Cake

People in a country called France make a special cake to remember the wise men. The cake is called *La Galette des Rois,* or Cake of the Kings. A bean or nut is baked into the cake. The person who finds the bean or nut in his or her piece of cake is declared king or queen of the party. Enjoy making a king's cake with your child. Remind your child that people all over the world are happy baby Jesus is born.

You will need:

    cake mix and ingredients   cake pan
    measuring utensils   one dried bean

Mix cake mix according to the directions. Pour the batter into the cake pan. Push the dried bean just under the surface of the batter. Bake as directed.

We are happy baby Jesus is born.

Reproducible 6A

Permission granted to photocopy for local church use. © 1998 Abingdon Press.

BibleZone™

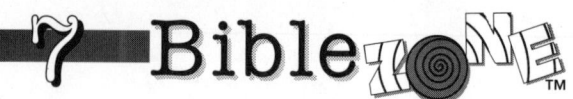

Talking to God

Enter the Zone

Bible Verse
Teach us to pray.
Luke 11:1

Bible Story
Matthew 6:9-15

Jesus was a man of prayer. He continually turned to God for the strength and power to carry out his ministry. Seeing Jesus' dependence on prayer, it is no wonder the disciples asked Jesus to teach them to pray. Jesus proceeded to teach his disciples how to pray the prayer we call the Lord's Prayer. In the first three petitions of the prayer, Jesus focused on God's nature, kingdom, and will. In the remaining petitions of the prayer, he focused on human needs—food, forgiveness, and freedom from evil. In providing a prayer on which to model our own prayer life, Jesus offers us a way to practice prayer as both a corporate and a personal spiritual discipline.

Jesus' use of the term *Father* invites all believers to share in a favored relationship with God through Jesus Christ. The Lord's Prayer itself is indicative of the balanced lifestyle that accompanies faithful discipleship. It addresses our relationship to God and to others, our physical and spiritual needs, and our earthly and eternal life. Praying to God is not just something to do when we are in need, feel bad or lost, or are participating in a worship ritual. Jesus taught us to pray with grateful hearts to a loving and forgiving God who guides, encourages, supports, and always cares for each of us.

Because of their limited verbal ability young children should not be expected to recite the Lord's Prayer in this lesson. However, young children delight in repetition, and they can begin to learn the prayer. Becoming familiar with the words of the Lord's Prayer allows preschoolers to participate more fully in worship.

More important to this lesson, however, is the example of Jesus. Because young children learn by imitation, it is important for children to know that not only did Jesus teach his friends to pray, but also that he prayed often. Children learn prayer not only from the example of Jesus, but also from examples of the adults in their lives. Pray often for and with the children in your class. Remember that your children come from a variety of backgrounds, and some may not have adult role models who pray. Consciously look for ways to incorporate prayer into your classroom time.

We can talk to God.

Scope the Zone

ZONE	TIME	SUPPLIES	ZILLIES™
Zoom Into the Zone			
Prayer Square	10 minutes	Reproducible 7A, scissors, empty cereal box, glue, construction paper	none
Prayer Square Says	5 minutes	prayer square (Reproducible 7A)	none
BibleZone™			
Do the Happy Hop	5 minutes	none	none
Talking to God	10 minutes	Reproducible 7A	none
Bible Verse Buzz	5 minutes	Bible, BZ Bee	none
Sing!	5 minutes	cassette player	Cassette
LifeZone			
Prayer Rubbings	10 minutes	tape, plain paper, crayons with papers removed	praying hands molds
Prayer Polka	10 minutes	Reproducible 7B, tape, cassette player	Cassette
Happy Talk	10 minutes	none	inflatable smile face

Zillies™ are found in the **BibleZone™ FUNspirational™ Kit.**

Zoom Into the Zone

Choose one or more activities to catch your children's interest.

Supplies:
Reproducible 7A, scissors, empty cereal box, glue, construction paper

Zillies™:
none

Prayer Square

Photocopy and cut out one copy of the prayer square face **(Reproducible 7A)**. Glue the square onto the front or back of an empty cereal box so that the opening of the cereal box is at the bottom of the prayer square face.

Cut four two-inch-wide strips of paper. Accordion fold each strip. Glue one strip on each side of the box to represent arms. Glue two strips at the bottom of the box to represent legs.

Show the children the prayer square. Cut paper into one-inch-wide strips. Let the children add hair to the square by gluing on the paper strips.

Say: Today our Bible story is about the time Jesus taught his friends how to pray. When we pray, we are talking to God. *(Show the children the prayer square puppet.)* This is Prayer Square. He will help us learn about talking to God.

 **We can talk to God.**

Supplies:
prayer square (Reproducible 7A)

Zillies™:
none

Prayer Square Says

Have the children move to an open area. Stand in front of the children, with the prayer square puppet **(Reproducible 7A)** on your hand.

Say: Let's play a game. Whenever I hold up Prayer Square and say, "Prayer Square says," I want you to do whatever Prayer Square tells you to do. If I don't hold up Prayer Square and don't say, "Prayer Square says," then don't do what I tell you to do.

Play the game with the children. Hold up the prayer square puppet each time you say, "Prayer Square says."

Prayer Square says clap your hands.
Prayer Square says touch your toes.
Nod your head.
Prayer Square says put your hands on your head.
Prayer Square says hop on one foot.
Touch your nose.
Prayer Square says turn around.
Stomp your feet.
Prayer Square says sit on the floor.

BibleZone™

Bible

Choose one or more activities to immerse your children in the Bible story.

Do the Happy Hop

Supplies:
none

Zillies™:
none

each the children the word *happy* in American Sign Language.

Open both hands with palms facing toward the chest. Pat the chest several times while moving the hands in an upward motion.

Use the following movement activity to lead your children to the story area.

The Happy Hop

Do the happy hop,
*(Stand still; sign the word **happy**.)*
Hop, hop, hop.
(Hop three times.)
Do the happy hop,
*(Stand still; sign the word **happy**.)*
Hop, hop, hop.
(Hop three times.)

Tell everyone we're happy today.
We're gonna learn what Jesus had to say.
(Stand still; shake index finger.)

Do the happy hop,
*(Stand still; sign the word **happy**.)*
Hop, hop, hop.
(Hop three times.)
Do the happy hop,
*(Stand still; sign the word **happy**.)*
Hop, hop, hop.
(Hop three times.)

Today we'll learn how he said to pray,
And we'll talk to God along the way.
(Stand still; fold hands in prayer.)

Do the happy hop,
*(Stand still; sign the word **happy**.)*
Hop, hop, hop.
(Hop three times.)
Do the happy hop,
*(Stand still; sign the word **happy**.)*
Hop, hop, hop.
(Hop three times.)

Bible Story

Talking to God

by Daphna Flegal

 *ave the children sit down in your story area. Show the children the prayer square puppet (**Reproducible 7A**). Use the puppet to tell the Bible story.*

My name is Prayer Square. I like to pray. That means I like to talk to God. In the morning when I first wake up, I pray, "Thank you, God, for this sunny day." Or maybe I pray, "Thank you, God, for this rainy day."

Sometimes I talk to God about how I feel. I pray, "I feel happy today. Thank you, God, for happy feelings." Or I pray, "I don't feel good today. Help me feel better soon."

When I eat my breakfast, I pray, "Thank you, God, for cereal and milk." What do you like to eat for breakfast? *(Encourage the children to respond.)* Then you can pray, "Thank you, God, for *(name the things the children named)*."

After breakfast I play with my friends. I pray, "Thank you, God, for friends." You are all my friends. "Thank you, God, for *(name each child)*."

At lunch time my friends and I sing a prayer. *(Sing to the tune of "London Bridge.")*

> Thank you, God, for food to eat,
> Food to eat, food to eat.
> Thank you, God, for food to eat.
> Amen. Amen.

After lunch I like to listen to a story from the Bible. The Bible is a special book that tells us about God and Jesus. The Bible tells us that Jesus talked to God. He thanked God for food. Jesus asked God to help him make sick people well. And he asked God to help him do hard things.

Jesus' friends saw Jesus talking to God. The friends asked Jesus to teach them how to talk to God. They said, "Jesus, teach us to pray."

Jesus taught his friends a special prayer. We call the prayer the Lord's Prayer. Listen while I say the prayer for you.

(Say this version of the Lord's Prayer, or repeat the version used by your church family.)

> Our Father in heaven,
>   hallowed be your name,
>   your kingdom come,
>   your will be done, on earth as in heaven.
> Give us today our daily bread.
> Forgive us our sins
>   as we forgive those who sin against us.
> Save us from the time of trial
>   and deliver us from evil.
> For the kingdom, the power, and the glory
>   are yours now and for ever. Amen.

English translation of The Lord's Prayer by the International Consultation on English Texts. From The United Methodist Hymnal, 894.

Zone In With BZ Bee

Bible Verse Buzz

Choose a child to hold the Bible open to Luke 11:1.

Say: Today our Bible story is the prayer Jesus taught his friends to pray. When we pray, we talk to God. We can talk to God.

Say the Bible verse, "Teach us to pray" (Luke 11:1), for the children. Have the children say the Bible verse after you.

Turn your back to the children or hide your hands underneath a table or behind the **BibleZone™ FUNspirational™ Kit** lid as you place the **BZ Bee puppet** (see page 174) on your hand. Turn around or bring the puppet out where the children can see it.

Pretend to make the puppet talk. Change your voice for the puppet:

Bzzz. Bzzz. Bzzz. Hi, everybody! I'm BZ Bee. *Bzzz. Bzzz. Bzzz.* I like to taste fingers. Do you have fingers? Yum, yum, yum. Let me taste.

Go to each child. Encourage, but do not force, each child to hold up his or her fingers. Have BZ pretend to taste each child's fingers. Have BZ say things like:

Mmmm. Mmmm. You taste like honey.
Bzzz. Bzzz. You taste like strawberries.
Yumm. Yumm. You taste like blueberries.

After BZ has tasted each child's fingers, say:

Bzzz. Bzzz. Bzzz. I like to taste your fingers. They're yummy. *(Rub BZ's stomach.)*

Bzzz. Bzzz. Bzzz. I like something else even more than fingers.

I like the Bible. *Bzzz. Bzzz. Bzzz.* You heard a Bible story today. Who taught his friends a special prayer? *(Jesus)* What do we call the special prayer Jesus taught his friends? *(the Lord's Prayer)*

Bzzz. Bzzz. Bzzz. Jesus taught his friends a special prayer called the Lord's Prayer. When we pray, we are talking to God.

We can talk to God.

Bzzz. Bzzz. Bzzz. Let's say the Bible verse together.

"Teach us to pray" (Luke 11:1).

Have the children repeat the Bible verse with BZ Bee.

Have BZ Bee say good-bye to the children. Put the puppet away.

Bible

Choose one or more activities to immerse your children in the Bible story.

Supplies:
cassette player

Zillies™:
Cassette

Sing!

ave the children stand in a circle. Play the song "God's Gotta Lotta Love" from the **Cassette**. Do the motions as suggested.

God's Gotta Lotta Love

God's gotta lotta love to go around,
(Walk around in a circle.)
go around, go around.
God's gotta lotta love to go around,
so sing a happy sound.
(Stop; cup hands around mouth.)
la la la la la la la

God's gotta lotta love to go around,
(Walk around in a circle.)
go around, go around.
God's gotta lotta love to go around,
so hum a happy sound.
(Stop; point to mouth.)
hm hm hm hm hm hm hm

God's gotta lotta love to go around,
(Walk around in a circle.)
go around, go around.
God's gotta lotta love to go around,
so whistle a happy sound.
(Stop; try to whistle.)
(whistle)

God's gotta lotta love to go around,
(Walk around in a circle.)
go around, go around.
God's gotta lotta love to go around,
so play a happy sound.
(Stop; pretend to play piano.)

God's gotta lotta love to go around,
(Walk around in a circle.)
go around, go around.
God's gotta lotta love to go around,
so shout a happy sound.
(Stop; wave hands above head.)
hip, hip, hooray, hip, hip, hooray

God's gotta lotta love to go around,
(Walk around in a circle.)
go around, go around.
God's gotta lotta love to go around,
so sing a happy sound.
(Stop; cup hands around mouth.)

Writers: Janet McMahan-Wilson and Dennis Scott
© 1991 John T. Benson Publishing Co. (ASCAP) (a div. of Brentwood-Benson Music Publishing, Inc.)
All rights reserved. Used by permission.

From the Brentwood-Benson Music Publishing, Inc. recording *Time Out To Sing*.

Choose one or more activities to bring the Bible to life.

Prayer Rubbings

Supplies: tape, plain paper, crayons with papers removed

Zillies™: praying hands molds

Lightly tape a **praying hands mold** to the table in front of each child. Tape a piece of plain paper over the mold. Show each child how to rub the side of a crayon (with paper removed) over the mold so that the outline of the praying hands shows through the paper. Retape the paper to allow the children to make more than one rubbing.

Say: Today our Bible story is about the time Jesus taught his friends how to pray. When we pray, we are talking to God. Sometimes when we talk to God, we fold our hands in prayer.

Prayer Polka

Supplies: Reproducible 7B, tape, cassette player

Zillies™: Cassette

Photocopy the praying hands picture **(Reproducible 7B)** for each child. Tape the pictures to the floor around the room. Play music from the **Cassette**. Have the children move around the room as the music plays. Stop the music. Have the children run quickly to stand on a praying hands picture when the music stops.

Say: Jesus' friends asked Jesus to "teach us to pray" (Luke 11:1).

Have the children repeat: **"Teach us to pray."**

Play the music again and have the children move around the room. Stop the music. Have the children run to a praying hands picture.

Say: When we pray, we talk to God. Let's talk to God right now. Let's pray, "Thank you, God, for Jesus."

Have the children repeat: **"Thank you, God, for Jesus."**

Play the music again and have the children move around the room. Stop the music. Have the children run to a praying hands picture.

Say: Let's pray, "Thank you, God, for friends."

Have the children repeat: **"Thank you, God, for friends."**

Continue the game as the children show interest. Add prayers thanking God for moms and dads, animals, food, church, families, and so forth.

Life Zone

Choose one or more activities to bring the Bible to life.

Supplies:
none

Zillies™:
inflatable smile face

Happy Talk

ave the children stand in a circle. Show the children the **inflatable smile face** doll.

Say: This is Happy. He is happy to be here with you.

Sing the song printed below to the tune of "Did You Ever See a Lassie?" Make the smile face doll do the suggested motions. Encourage the children to copy the motions.

If you're feeling happy,
So happy, so happy,
If you're feeling happy,
Then wiggle your hands.
*(Shake the doll's hands.
Have the children shake their hands.)*

Wiggle and wiggle
And wiggle and wiggle.
If you're feeling happy,
Then wiggle your hands.

If you're feeling happy,
So happy, so happy,
If you're feeling happy,
Then shake out your foot.
*(Shake one of the doll's feet.
Have the children shake one foot.)*

Shaking and shaking
And shaking and shaking.
If you're feeling happy,
Then shake out your foot.

If you're feeling happy,
So happy, so happy,
If you're feeling happy,
Then turn all around.
*(Turn the doll around.
Have the children turn around.)*

Turning and turning
And turning and turning.
If you're feeling happy,
Then turn all around.

If you're feeling happy,
So happy, so happy,
If you're feeling happy,
Then jump up and down.
*(Move the doll up and down.
Have the children jump up and down.)*

Jumping and jumping
And jumping and jumping.
If you're feeling happy,
Then jump up and down.

Say: Happy has something special to tell each one of you.

Call the children to come up one at a time. Let each child hug the smile face doll. As the child hugs the doll, **say:** *(Child's name),* **God loves you.**

Say: I'm happy that we can talk to God. Let's talk to God right now. Thank you, God, for *(name each child in your class.)*

Photocopy the **HomeZone**™ newsletter to send home to parents.

Home Zone For Parents

Bible Verse
Teach us to pray.
Luke 11:1

Bible Story
Matthew 6:9-15

Talking With God

Today your child heard the Bible story of the time when Jesus' friends asked Jesus to teach them to pray. Jesus responded by teaching his friends the prayer we call the Lord's Prayer. With this prayer Jesus teaches us to pray with grateful hearts to a loving and forgiving God who guides, encourages, supports, and always cares for each of us.

Children learn to talk to God not only from the example of Jesus, but also from examples of the adults in their lives. Pray often for and with your child. Consciously look for ways to incorporate prayer into your daily life.

Pray With Your Child

- Help your child understand prayer as simply talking to God. Let your child hear you talking to God. When your child sees that prayer is an everyday habit in your life, it can become a natural part of your child's life.

- Say a blessing before each meal. Keep the prayers simple.

- Give thanks to God anytime. Say impromptu prayers in the midst of everyday activities.

- As your child grows, so will his or her understanding of prayer. Simple bedtime prayers of thanks can expand into prayers that ask for help, say "I'm sorry," or seek comfort.

- Reassure your child that God is always with us and always hears our prayers. Let your child know by example that talking to God is an important part of life.

© 1995 Cokesbury.

We can talk to God.

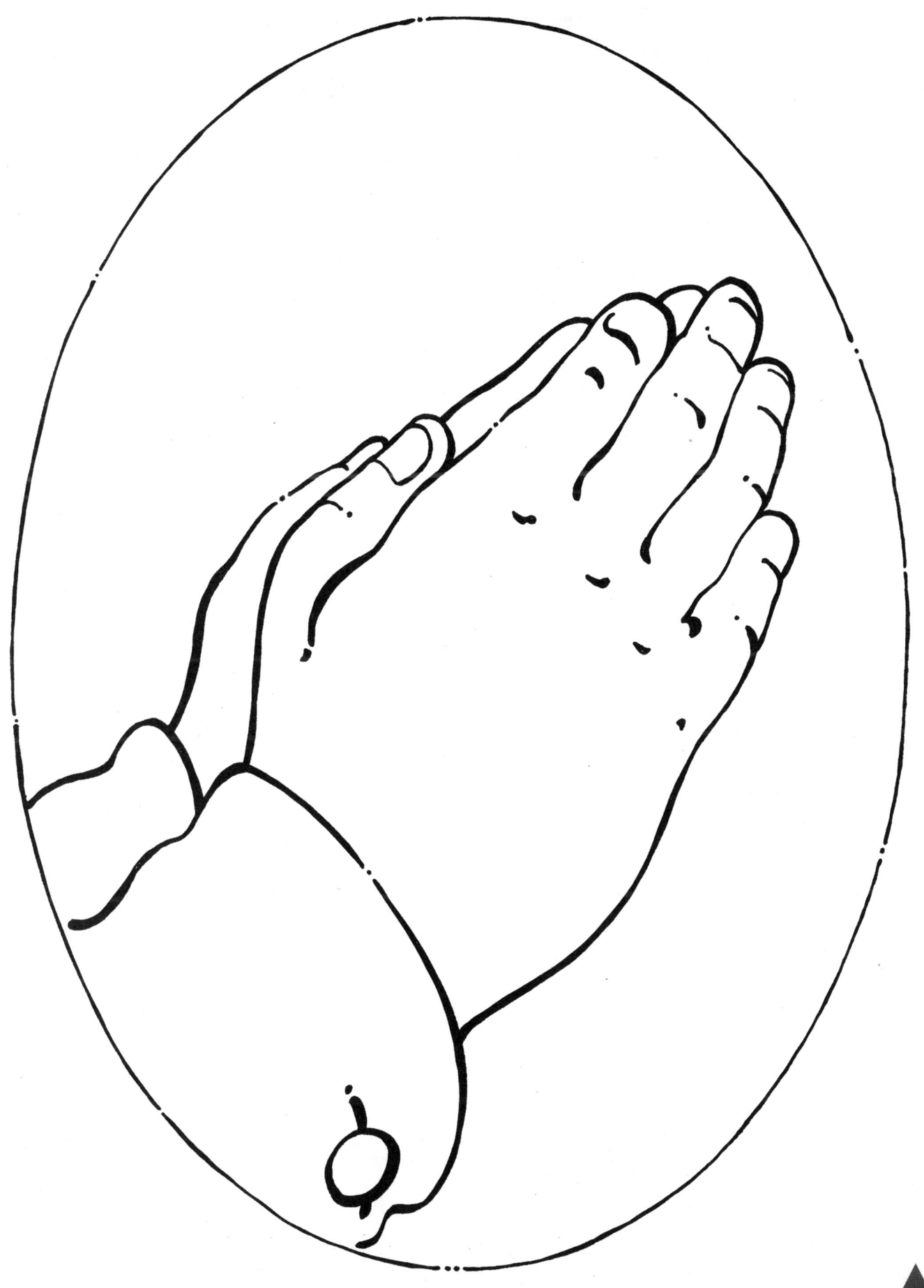

8 Bible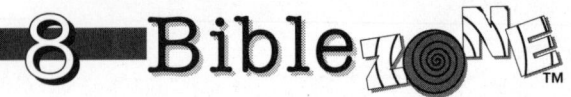

A Beatitude Attitude

Enter the

Bible Verse
Be happy and glad.
Matthew 5:12, *Good News Bible*

Bible Story
Matthew 5: 1-12

The Scripture reference for today is a collection of brief blessings and sayings that are more commonly known as the Beatitudes. The Beatitudes are part of a longer text known as the Sermon on the Mount. The Sermon on the Mount also is found in a shorter version in the Book of Luke.

The Beatitudes, the first twelve verses, express a paradoxical world. These sayings of Jesus forced persons to rethink their most basic reactions. The kingdom of God as explained by Jesus is the reverse of the world as it appears to the average person. People usually return aggressive behavior with equally aggressive behavior. Wealth and accumulation of material goods are not only respected, but desired. Humbleness and meekness are considered traits to be taken advantage of.

Jesus' teachings brought a new emphasis. This is not the way things are in the kingdom of God. Jesus offered hope to those in the world who had known suffering and loss. Jesus' message was that God's goodness is for all people.

Young children do not yet have the higher-level thinking skills necessary to understand the contradictions of Jesus' teachings. The goal in this lesson is to show the children that Jesus was a special teacher who taught about God; to introduce the Beatitudes; and to help children have happy experiences at church. Even young children can feel the joy that knowing that God loves them can bring.

We are happy to hear Jesus' teachings.

Scope the Zone

ZONE	TIME	SUPPLIES	ZILLIES™
Zoom Into the Zone			
Happy Stick	10 minutes	Reproducible 8A, scissors, crayons; glue, paper plate; paper towel, ruler, or paint stirrer	none
Happy Feet	10 minutes	mural paper or large construction paper, tape, crayons	none
BibleZone™			
Do the Happy Hop	5 minutes	none	none
Happy Teachings	10 minutes	happy stick (Reproducible 8A)	none
Bible Verse Buzz	5 minutes	Bible, BZ Bee	none
Sing!	5 minutes	cassette player	Cassette, kazoos
LifeZone			
Happy Hands	5 minutes	none	none
Happy Hero Hop	15 minutes	Reproducible 8B, scissors, tape, crayons	none
Happy Talk	10 minutes	none	inflatable smile face

Zillies™ are found in the **BibleZone™ FUNspirational™ Kit.**

Zoom Into the Zone

Choose one or more activities to catch your children's interest.

Supplies:
Reproducible 8A, scissors, crayons; glue, paper plate; paper towel roll, ruler, or paint stirrer

Zillies™:
none

Happy Stick

hotocopy and cut out one copy of the happy face **(Reproducible 8A)**. Let the first children who arrive work together to decorate the happy face. Glue the happy face onto a paper plate. Glue or tape a paper towel roll, ruler, or paint stirrer (usually obtained free from paint stores or paint departments at discount stores) to the back of the paper plate to make a handle.

Say: Today our Bible story is about some of the things Jesus taught his friends.

> **We are happy to hear Jesus' teachings.**

Plan to use the happy stick during the Bible story.

Supplies:
mural paper or large construction paper, tape, crayons

Zillies™:
none

Happy Feet

ape mural paper or several pieces of large construction paper on the wall near the floor. Have enough paper mounted for each child to be able to sit in front of a portion of paper.

Say: Today our Bible story is about some of the things Jesus taught his friends.

> **We are happy to hear Jesus' teachings.**

I want you to make happy pictures to help us remember that we are happy to hear Jesus' teachings. And I want you to draw these pictures in a silly, happy way—I want you to use your feet!

Have each child take off one shoe and one sock. Have the children sit down in front of the paper with their feet to the wall. Let each child choose a crayon. Have each child put the crayon between her or his first two toes and color on the paper.

If you have children that do not want to take off their shoes and socks, let those children lie down on their stomachs and color with their hands.

BIBLEZONE™

Bible

Choose one or more activities to immerse your children in the Bible story.

Do the Happy Hop

Teach the children the word *happy* in American Sign Language.

Open both hands with palms facing toward the chest. Pat the chest several times while moving the hands in an upward motion.

Use the following movement activity to lead your children to the story area.

Supplies:
none

Zillies™:
none

The Happy Hop

Do the happy hop,
*(Stand still; sign the word **happy**.)*
Hop, hop, hop.
(Hop three times.)
Do the happy hop,
*(Stand still; sign the word **happy**.)*
Hop, hop, hop.
(Hop three times.)

Tell everyone we're happy today.
We're gonna learn what Jesus had to say.
(Stand still; shake index finger.)

Do the happy hop,
*(Stand still; sign the word **happy**.)*
Hop, hop, hop.
(Hop three times.)
Do the happy hop,
*(Stand still; sign the word **happy**.)*
Hop, hop, hop.
(Hop three times.)

Today we'll learn how he said to be glad.
And we'll tell what we learn to our moms and dads.
*(Stand still; sign the word **happy**.)*

Do the happy hop,
*(Stand still; sign the word **happy**.)*
Hop, hop, hop.
(Hop three times.)
Do the happy hop,
*(Stand still; sign the word **happy**.)*
Hop, hop, hop.
(Hop three times.)

Bible Zone Story

Happy Teachings

by Daphna Flegal

ave the children sit down in your story area. Show the children the happy stick (**Reproducible 8A**).

Say: I want each of you to help me tell the story today. I will give you the happy stick to hold when it is your turn to talk.

Let's think about being happy. When are you happy? Are you happy when your mother gives you a hug? Are you happy when you eat ice cream? Are you happy when you stay up past your bedtime? *(Child's name), when are you happy? (Give the happy stick to the child named. Let the child respond to your question. Give the stick to other children and let them respond to the question.)*

Do you feel happy when you go someplace special? When you go to your grandparents home? When you go to a friend's house? When you go to church? *(Child's name), where do you go that makes you feel happy? (Give the happy stick to the child named. Let the child respond to your question. Give the stick to other children and let them respond to the question.)*

What do you do when you feel happy? Do you laugh? Do you smile? Do you jump up and down? *(Child's name), what do you do when you feel happy? (Give the happy stick to the child named. Let the child respond to your question. Give the stick to other children and let them respond to the question.)*

Do you have someone you like to be with when you feel happy? Is it your friend? Your mom or dad? Your brother or sister? *(Child's name), who do you like to be with when you feel happy? (Give the happy stick to the child named. Let the child respond to your question. Make sure every child has had a turn holding the stick and answering at least one question.)*

Jesus' friends wanted to be with Jesus. They were happy to listen to Jesus teach about God. One day Jesus sat down with his friends and said:

Happy are people who trust God.

Happy are people when they are sad and God helps them feel better.

Happy are people who do not think they are most important.

Happy are people who do what God wants them to do.

Happy are people who forgive others.

Happy are people who love God.

Happy are people who work for peace.

Be happy and glad!

In With BZ Bee

Bible Verse Buzz

hoose a child to hold the Bible open to Matthew 5:12.

Say: Today our Bible story was about some of the things Jesus taught his friends. Jesus told his friends to "Be happy and glad."

Say the Bible verse, "Be happy and glad" (Matthew 5:12, *Good News Bible*), for the children. Have the children say the Bible verse after you.

Turn your back to the children or hide your hands underneath a table or behind the **BibleZone™ FUNspirational™ Kit** lid as you place the **BZ Bee puppet** (see page 174) on your hand. Turn around or bring the puppet out where the children can see it.

Pretend to make the puppet talk. Change your voice for the puppet:

Bzzz. Bzzz. Bzzz. Hi, everybody! I'm BZ Bee. *Bzzz. Bzzz. Bzzz.* I like to taste fingers. Do you have fingers? Yum, yum, yum. Let me taste.

Go to each child. Encourage, but do not force, each child to hold up his or her fingers. Have BZ pretend to taste each child's fingers. Have BZ say things like:

Mmmm. Mmmm. You taste like honey.
Bzzz. Bzzz. You taste like strawberries.
Yumm. Yumm. You taste like blueberries.

After BZ has tasted each child's fingers, say:

Bzzz. Bzzz. Bzzz. I like to taste your fingers. They're yummy. *(Rub BZ's stomach.)*

Bzzz. Bzzz. Bzzz. I like something else even more than fingers.

I like the Bible. *Bzzz. Bzzz. Bzzz.* You heard a Bible story today. Who taught his friends about God? *(Jesus)* What did Jesus tell his friends? *(Be happy and glad.)*

Bzzz. Bzzz. Bzzz. Jesus taught his friends about God. He told his friends to be happy and glad.

 **We are happy to hear Jesus' teachings.**

Bzzz. Bzzz. Bzzz. Let's say the Bible verse together.

"Be happy and glad" (Matthew 5:12, *Good News Bible*).

Have the children repeat the Bible verse with BZ Bee.

Have BZ Bee say good-bye to the children. Put the puppet away.

Bible

Choose one or more activities to immerse your children in the Bible story.

Supplies:
cassette player

Zillies™:
Cassette, kazoos

Sing!

Say: Today our Bible story is about some of the things Jesus taught his friends. One of the things Jesus taught is that we should love one another.

Give each child a **kazoo**. Play the song "This Is My Commandment" from the **Cassette**. Let the children play their kazoos with the music.

NOTE: Wash the kazoos in soap and water before using them again.

This Is My Commandment

This is My commandment,
That you love one another,
That your joy may be full.
This is My commandment,
That you love one another,
That your joy may be full.

That your joy may be full,
That your joy may be full.
This is My commandment,
That you love one another,
That your joy may be full.

That your joy may be full,
That your joy may be full.
This is My commandment,
That you love one another,
That your joy may be full.
That your joy may be full!

Text: John 15:12
Music: Traditional

Arr. © 1986 New Spring Publishing, Inc. (ASCAP) (a div. of Brentwood-Benson Music Publishing, Inc.)
All rights reserved. Used by permission.
(Arrangement copyright refers and applies to recorded music on audiocassette.)

From the Brentwood Music, Inc. recording *Kids Sing Praise vol. 1.*

Life

Choose one or more activities to bring the Bible to life.

Happy Hands

Have the children sit down on the floor.

Say: Listen carefully as I sing a song. If you are wearing something that is the color I name, stand up. When I ask you to "tell me that you're happy," sign the word happy (see p. 97) **with your hands.**

Sing the following song to the tune of "Are You Sleeping?"

Who's wearing yellow?
Who's wearing yellow?
Please stand up.
(Children wearing yellow stand up.)
Please stand up.

Tell me that you're happy.
(Sign the word happy.)
Tell me that you're happy.
Sit back down.
Sit back down.

Sing the song and name different colors until everyone has had at least one turn to stand up.

Say: Our Bible story is about some of the things Jesus taught his friends.

 **We are happy to hear Jesus' teachings.**

Supplies:
none

Zillies™:
none

Happy Hero Hop

Photocopy and cut out the triangle **(Reproducible 8B)** for each child. Let the children color the triangle with crayons. Tape the triangle onto the front of each child's clothing. Have the children sit down in an open area of the room.

Say: One of the things Jesus taught his friends was that people who do what God wants them to do are happy. If I say something that you think God wants us to do, jump up, show me your happy badge, and say, "Be happy and glad!"

Share your toys. (Jump.)
Be happy and glad!

Take turns. (Jump.)
Be happy and glad!

Be kind. (Jump.)
Be happy and glad!

Show love. (Jump.)
Be happy and glad!

Supplies:
Reproducible 8B, scissors, tape, crayons

Zillies™:
none

PRESCHOOL 6

Choose one or more activities to bring the Bible to life.

Supplies:
none

Zillies™:
inflatable smile face

Happy Talk

ave the children stand in a circle. Show the children the **inflatable smile face** doll.

Say: This is Happy. He is happy to be here with you.

Sing the song printed below to the tune of "Did You Ever See a Lassie?" Make the smile face doll do the suggested motions. Encourage the children to copy the motions.

If you're feeling happy,
So happy, so happy,
If you're feeling happy,
Then wiggle your hands.
*(Shake the doll's hands.
Have the children shake their hands.)*

Wiggle and wiggle
And wiggle and wiggle.
If you're feeling happy,
Then wiggle your hands.

If you're feeling happy,
So happy, so happy,
If you're feeling happy,
Then shake out your foot.
*(Shake one of the doll's feet.
Have the children shake one foot.)*

Shaking and shaking
And shaking and shaking.
If you're feeling happy,
Then shake out your foot.

If you're feeling happy,
So happy, so happy,
If you're feeling happy,
Then turn all around.
*(Turn doll around.
Have the children turn around.)*

Turning and turning
And turning and turning.
If you're feeling happy,
Then turn all around.

If you're feeling happy,
So happy, so happy,
If you're feeling happy,
Then jump up and down.
*(Move the doll up and down.
Have the children jump up and down.)*

Jumping and jumping
And jumping and jumping.
If you're feeling happy,
Then jump up and down.

Say: Happy has something special to tell each one of you.

Call the children to come up one at a time. Let each child hug the smile face doll. As the child hugs the doll, **say: *(Child's name)*, God loves you.**

Say: I'm happy that we can talk to God. Let's talk to God right now. Thank you, God, for *(name each child in your class)*.

Photocopy the **HomeZone**™ newsletter to send home to parents.

Home Zone For Parents

A Beatitude Attitude

Today your child heard the Bible story of when Jesus taught his friends the Beatitudes. The Beatitudes are brief blessings and sayings that were included in the Sermon on the Mount.

Young children do not yet have the higher-level thinking skills necessary to fully understand the Beatitudes. The goal in this lesson is to show the children that Jesus was a special teacher who taught about God; to introduce the Beatitudes; and to help children have happy experiences at church. Even young children can feel the joy that comes from knowing that God loves them.

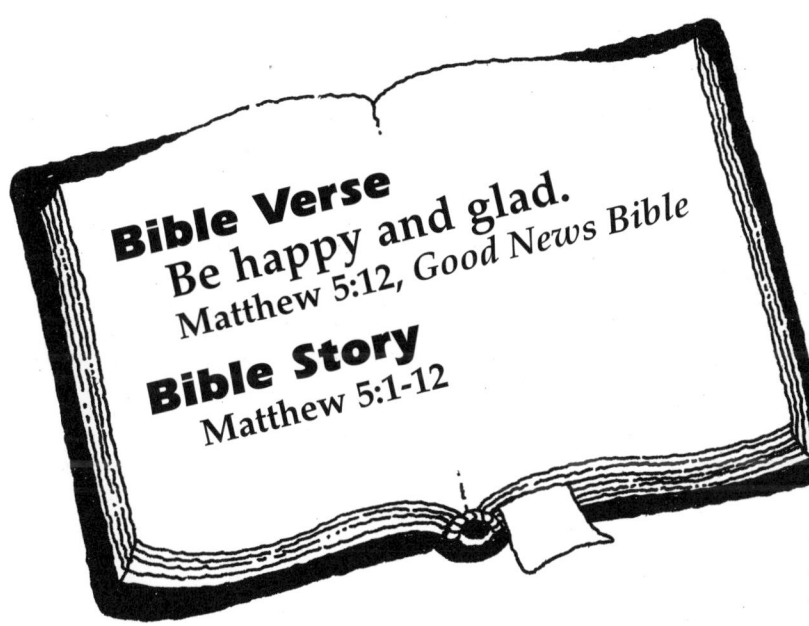

Bible Verse
Be happy and glad.
Matthew 5:12, Good News Bible

Bible Story
Matthew 5:1-12

The Beatitudes

(paraphrased for use with young children)

Happy are people who trust God.

Happy are people when they are sad and God helps them feel better.

Happy are people who do not think they are most important.

Happy are people who do what God wants them to do.

Happy are people who forgive others.

Happy are people who love God.

Happy are people who work for peace.

Be Happy Cake

Enjoy making this happy dessert with your child. Remind your child that Jesus taught us to "be happy and glad" (Matthew 5:12, *Good News Bible*).

cake mix
chocolate sandwich cookies
yellow frosting
   or white frosting and yellow food coloring
round cake pan
M&M candies

Bake the cake according to the directions, in a round cake pan. Let the cake cool. Remove the cake from the pan and place on a platter. Frost the cake with yellow frosting. (You may make yellow frosting by mixing yellow food coloring into white frosting.) Press half of a sandwich cookie into the frosting to make each eye. Use M&M candies to make the smile.

We are happy to hear Jesus' teachings.

Reproducible 8A

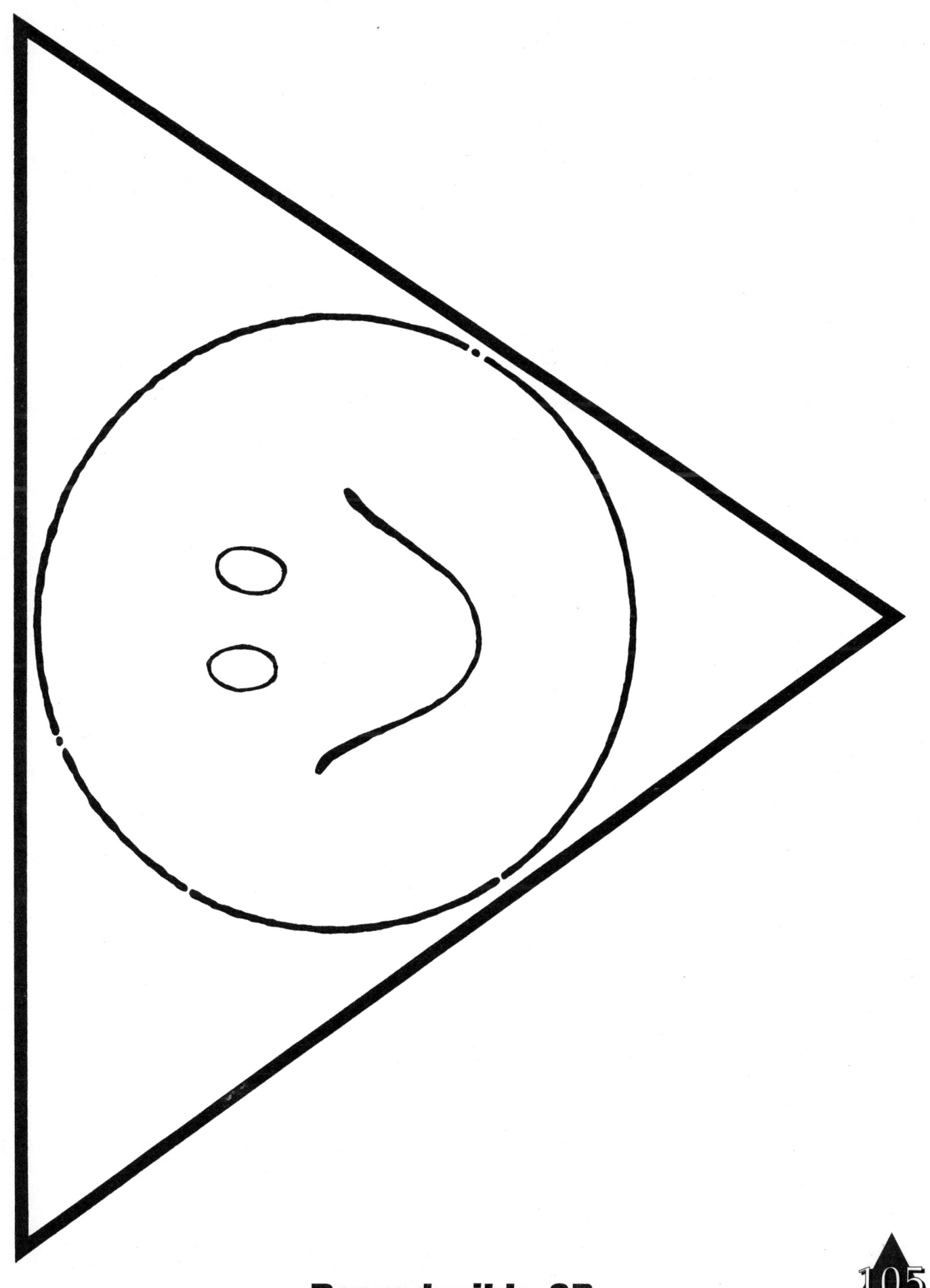

9 Bible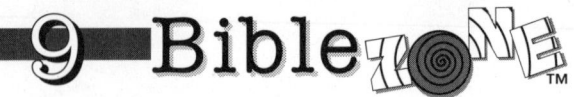

The Great Commandment

Enter the

Bible Verse
Love the Lord your God with all your heart.
Matthew 22:37, *Good News Bible*

Bible Story
Matthew 22:35-40

In the Great Commandments in Matthew 22:35-40, Jesus combined Deuteronomy 6:5, called the Shema, and Leviticus 19:18b. Jesus' answer, as so often happened, came in response to a question, this time from a Pharisaic lawyer who was trying to test Jesus. "Teacher," the lawyer asked, "which commandment in the law is greatest?"

The question of which was the greatest commandment seems to have been raised often by the rabbis. The content of Jesus' answer was not new—what was new was how he redefined how we should love God. Love for God manifests itself not only in following the law, but also in expanding our love to others. If we love God, we will love our neighbors; when we show love to our neighbors, we also are showing love to God.

The children you teach should experience love through faithful and caring relationships with their parents, family members, teachers, and caregivers. It is important to explain love to children with specific examples of ways that we show love.

Young children also need the love for self that Jesus describes as the measure of loving actions toward others. Ironically, your children's self-love is learned from observing and experiencing love shown by significant adults in their worlds. Their self-image is determined largely by messages they receive about themselves early in life. These messages will have a long-lasting impact on their ability to give and to receive love. Each time you teach, think of specific ways that you can share God's love with your children.

We can love God and others.

Scope the

ZONE	TIME	SUPPLIES	ZILLIES™
Zoom Into the Zone			
Heartlines	5 minutes	Reproducible 9A, scissors	none
All Your Heart	10 minutes	mural paper or large construction paper, scissors, pencil, crayons or markers, glue or tape	none
BibleZone™			
Do the Happy Hop	5 minutes	none	none
The Greatest Rules	10 minutes	none	none
Bible Verse Buzz	5 minutes	Bible, BZ Bee	none
Sing!	5 minutes	cassette player	Cassette, kazoos
LifeZone			
Hip-Hop Hearts	10 minutes	Reproducibles 9A and 9B, scissors, tape	none
Happy Talk	10 minutes	none	inflatable smile face

Zillies™ are found in the **BibleZone™ FUNspirational™ Kit.**

Zoom Into the Zone

Choose one or more activities to catch your children's interest.

Supplies:
Reproducible 9A, scissors

Zillies™:
none

Heartlines

Photocopy and cut apart at least two copies of the hearts (**Reproducible 9A**). Place the hearts on the table or rug. Let the children take turns sorting the hearts by size. Then have the children line the hearts up from smallest to largest.

Say: Today our Bible story is about when Jesus taught his friends about love. Jesus told his friends to love God and to love one another.

We can love God and others.

Supplies:
mural paper or large construction paper, scissors, pencil, crayons or markers, glue or tape

Zillies™:
none

All Your Heart

Cut a large heart shape out of mural paper or large construction paper. Cut the heart into separate puzzle pieces. Make sure you have one piece for each child. Mark the pieces on the back with a pencil so that you can easily put the heart back together.

Give each child a heart puzzle piece. Let each child decorate his or her piece with crayons or markers. When the children are finished decorating, help them put their pieces together to make the whole heart. Glue the pieces to mural paper or tape the pieces on a door or wall.

Say: Today our Bible story is about when Jesus taught his friends about love. Jesus told his friends to love God and to love one another. Jesus said, "Love the Lord your God with all your heart" (Matthew 22:37, *Good News Bible*) and "Love your neighbor as you love yourself" (Matthew 22:39, *Good News Bible*).

Have the children repeat the Bible verse, "Love the Lord your God with all your heart" (Matthew 22:37, *Good News Bible*).

We can love God and others.

Choose one or more activities to immerse your children in the Bible story.

Do the Happy Hop

 each the children the word *happy* in American Sign Language.

Open both hands with palms facing toward the chest. Pat the chest several times while moving the hands in an upward motion.

Use the following movement activity to lead your children to the story area.

Supplies:
none

Zillies™:
none

The Happy Hop

Do the happy hop,
*(Stand still; sign the word **happy**.)*
Hop, hop, hop.
(Hop three times.)
Do the happy hop,
*(Stand still; sign the word **happy**.)*
Hop, hop, hop.
(Hop three times.)

Tell everyone we're happy today.
We're gonna learn what Jesus had to say.
(Stand still; shake index finger.)

Do the happy hop,
*(Stand still; sign the word **happy**.)*
Hop, hop, hop.
(Hop three times.)
Do the happy hop,
*(Stand still; sign the word **happy**.)*
Hop, hop, hop.
(Hop three times.)

Today we'll learn to love God and others.
And we'll share this love with our sisters and brothers.
(Stand still; cross hands over heart.)

Do the happy hop,
*(Stand still; sign the word **happy**.)*
Hop, hop, hop.
(Hop three times.)
Do the happy hop,
Stand still; sign the word **happy**.)
Hop, hop, hop.
(Hop three times.)

Bible Zone Story

The Greatest Rules

by Lorri Coates and Barbara McKone

ave the children stand in a circle. Tell the children the story and do the suggested motions.

One day a man asked Jesus which of God's rules was the most important rule of all.

Jesus answered, "You shall love the Lord your God with all your heart, *(place hands over heart)* and with all your soul, *(move arms in an arc around body)* and with all your mind." *(Touch palms to top of head.)* Jesus told the man that this was the first, and greatest, rule.

Let's say that important rule together. *(Say one line and do the motion; have the children repeat.)* "You shall love the Lord your God with all your heart, *(place hands over heart)* and with all your soul, *(move arms in an arc around body)* and with all your mind." *(Touch palms to top of head.)*

Jesus said that another of God's rules was like the first. "You shall love *(place hands over heart)* your neighbor *(point to others)* as yourself." *(Point to self.)* Jesus wanted us to remember that everyone else is as important as we are, and we should treat everyone with God's love.

Let's say that important rule together. *(Say one line and do the motion; have the children repeat.)* "You shall love *(Place hands over heart.)* your neighbor *(Point to others.)* as yourself." *(Point to self.)*

Let's learn a little verse to help us remember the greatest rules of all. Do you all know how to clap? Show me. Do you all know how to stomp? Show me that too.

(Demonstrate twice, then let the children follow.)
You shall love the Lord your God
(Shake finger in a fun way.)
With your heart and soul and mind, *(Clap, clap.)*
And to others that you know,
(Shake finger in a fun way.)
Be good, *(Clap, clap.)*
And kind! *(Stomp, stomp.)*
Be good, *(Clap, clap.)*
And kind! *(Stomp, stomp.)*

I'd like to do that again, this time with you. Will you try?

You shall love the Lord your God
(Shake finger in a fun way.)
With your heart and soul and mind, *(Clap, clap.)*
And to others that you know,
(Shake finger in a fun way.)
Be good, *(Clap, clap.)*
And kind! *(Stomp, stomp.)*
Be good, *(Clap, clap.)*
And kind! *(Stomp, stomp.)*

Zone In With BZ Bee

Bible Verse Buzz

Choose a child to hold the Bible open to Matthew 22:37.

Say: Today our Bible story is about two important rules Jesus taught about love. Jesus said to love God and to love one another.

Say the Bible verse, "Love the Lord your God with all your heart" (Matthew 22:37, *Good News Bible*), for the children. Have the children say the Bible verse after you.

Turn your back to the children or hide your hands underneath a table or behind the **BibleZone™ FUNspirational™ Kit** lid as you place the **BZ Bee puppet** (see page 174) on your hand. Turn around or bring the puppet out where the children can see it.

Pretend to make the puppet talk. Change your voice for the puppet:

Bzzz. Bzzz. Bzzz. Hi, everybody! I'm BZ Bee. *Bzzz. Bzzz. Bzzz.* I like to taste fingers. Do you have fingers? Yum, yum, yum. Let me taste.

Go to each child. Encourage, but do not force, each child to hold up his or her fingers. Have BZ pretend to taste each child's fingers. Have BZ say things like:

Mmmm. Mmmm. You taste like honey.
Bzzz. Bzzz. You taste like strawberries.
Yumm. Yumm. You taste like blueberries.

After BZ has tasted each child's fingers, say:

Bzzz. Bzzz. Bzzz. I like to taste your fingers. They're yummy. *(Rub BZ's stomach.)*

Bzzz. Bzzz. Bzzz. I like something else even more than fingers.

I like the Bible. *Bzzz. Bzzz. Bzzz.* You heard a Bible story today. Who taught his friends two important rules about love *(Jesus)* What did Jesus tell his friends? *(to love God and one another)*

Bzzz. Bzzz. Bzzz. Jesus taught his friends two important rules about love. Jesus said to love God with all your heart; and to love your neighbor as yourself.

 **We can love God and others.**

Bzzz. Bzzz. Bzzz. Let's say the Bible verse together.

"Love the Lord your God with all your heart" (Matthew 22:37, *Good News Bible*).

Have the children repeat the Bible verse with BZ Bee.

Have BZ Bee say good-bye to the children. Put the puppet away.

Bible

Choose one or more activities to immerse your children in the Bible story.

Supplies:
cassette player

Zillies™:
Cassette, kazoos

Sing!

Say: Today our Bible story is about some of the things Jesus taught his friends. One of the things Jesus taught is that we should love one another.

Give each child a **kazoo.** Play the song "This Is My Commandment" from the **Cassette.** Let the children play their kazoos with the music.

NOTE: Wash the kazoos in soap and water before using them again.

This Is My Commandment

This is My commandment,
That you love one another,
That your joy may be full.
This is My commandment,
That you love one another,
That your joy may be full.

That your joy may be full,
That your joy may be full.
This is My commandment,
That you love one another,
That your joy may be full.

That your joy may be full,
That your joy may be full.
This is My commandment,
That you love one another,
That your joy may be full.
That your joy may be full!

Text: John 15:12
Music: Traditional
Arr. © 1986 New Spring Publishing, Inc. (ASCAP) (a div. of Brentwood-Benson Music Publishing, Inc.)
All rights reserved. Used by permission.
(Arrangement copyright refers and applies to recorded music on audiocassette.)

From the Brentwood Music, Inc. recording *Kids Sing Praise vol. 1.*

Choose one or more activities to bring the Bible to life.

Hip-Hop Hearts

Photocopy and cut apart the mouth, ears, hands, and feet pictures (Reproducible 9B). Photocopy and cut out one of the heart pictures (Reproducible 9A). Have the children sit in your story area. Show the children the pictures and have them name each body part.

Say: Jesus taught us to love God with all our hearts, and souls, and mind.

Tape a body part picture in each corner of the room. Tape the heart in your story area. Make sure the children know where you are putting each of the pictures.

Say: When I call out the name of one of the pictures, jump up and hop to that picture. When you get to the picture, touch whatever I name on your own body. When I say our Bible verse, "Love the Lord your God with all your heart" (Matthew 22:37, *Good News Bible*), hop to the heart picture. Cross your hands over your heart and say the Bible verse after me.

Love God with your ears. *(Have the children hop to the ear picture. When the children reach the picture, have the children touch their ears.)*

Love the Lord your God with all your heart. *(Have the children hop to the heart picture, cross their hands over their hearts, and repeat the Bible verse.)*

Love God with your feet. *(Have the children hop to the feet picture. When the children reach the picture, have the children touch their feet.)*

Love the Lord your God with all your heart. *(Have the children hop to the heart picture, cross their hands over their hearts, and repeat the Bible verse.)*

Love God with your mouth. *(Have the children hop to the mouth picture. When the children reach the picture, have the children touch their mouths.)*

Love the Lord your God with all your heart. *(Have the children hop to the heart picture, cross their hands over their hearts, and repeat the Bible verse.)*

Love God with your hands. *(Have the children hop to the hands picture. When the children reach the picture, have the children clap their hands.)*

Love the Lord your God with all your heart. *(Have the children hop to the heart picture, cross their hands over their hearts, and repeat the Bible verse.)*

Supplies:
Reproducibles 9A and 9B, scissors, tape

Zillies™:
none

We can love God and others.

Life Zone

Choose one or more activities to bring the Bible to life.

Supplies:
none

Zillies™:
inflatable smile face

Happy Talk

 Have the children stand in a circle. Show the children the **inflatable smile face** doll.

Say: This is Happy. He is happy to be here with you.

Sing the song printed below to the tune of "Did You Ever See a Lassie?" Make the smile face doll do the suggested motions. Encourage the children to copy the motions.

If you're feeling happy,
So happy, so happy,
If you're feeling happy,
Then wiggle your hands.
(Shake the doll's hands.
Have the children shake their hands.)

Wiggle and wiggle
And wiggle and wiggle.
If you're feeling happy,
Then wiggle your hands.

If you're feeling happy,
So happy, so happy,
If you're feeling happy,
Then shake out your foot.
(Shake one of the doll's feet.
Have the children shake one foot.)

Shaking and shaking
And shaking and shaking.
If you're feeling happy,
Then shake out your foot.

If you're feeling happy,
So happy, so happy,
If you're feeling happy,
Then turn all around.
(Turn doll around.
Have the children turn around.)

Turning and turning
And turning and turning.
If you're feeling happy,
Then turn all around.

If you're feeling happy,
So happy, so happy,
If you're feeling happy,
Then jump up and down.
(Move the doll up and down.
Have the children jump up and down.)

Jumping and jumping
And jumping and jumping.
If you're feeling happy,
Then jump up and down.

Say: Happy has something special to tell each one of you.

Call the children to come up one at a time. Let each child hug the smile face doll. As the child hugs the doll, **say:** *(Child's name)*, **God loves you.**

Say: I'm happy that we can talk to God. Let's talk to God right now. Thank you, God, for *(name each child in your class).*

Photocopy the **HomeZone**™ newsletter to send home to parents.

Home Zone For Parents

Bible Verse
Love the Lord your God with all your heart.
Matthew 22:37, *Good News Bible*

Bible Story
Matthew 22:35-40

The Great Commandment

Today your child learned two important rules Jesus taught his friends. These rules are known as the Great Commandment. For the first rule Jesus quoted from Deuteronomy 6:5, "Love the Lord your God with all your heart, with all your soul, and with all your might" (Matthew 22:37, *Good News Bible*). For the second rule Jesus quotes from Leviticus 19:18, "Love your neighbors as you love yourself" (Matthew 22:39, *Good News Bible*).

The content of Jesus' answer was not new—what was new was how he redefined how we should love God. Love for God manifests itself not only in following the law, but also in expanding our love to others. If we love God, we will love our neighbors; when we show love to our neighbors, we also are showing love to God.

Children experience love through faithful and caring relationships with their parents, family members, teachers, and caregivers. Even their self-love is learned from love shown by significant adults in their worlds. Their self-image is determined largely by messages they receive about themselves early in life. These messages will have a long-lasting impact on their ability to give and receive love.

Waffle Hearts

frozen waffles
heart-shaped cookie cutter
powdered sugar

Cook frozen waffles according to the directions. Help your child use a heart-shaped cookie cutter to cut the waffles into heart shapes. Let your child decorate the waffles with powdered sugar.

Remind your child that Jesus taught us to love God with all our hearts. Jesus also taught us to love others.

While you enjoy eating the waffles with your child, be sure to say, "I love you!"

We can love God and others.

Reproducible 9A

Permission granted to photocopy for local church use. © 1998 Abingdon Press.

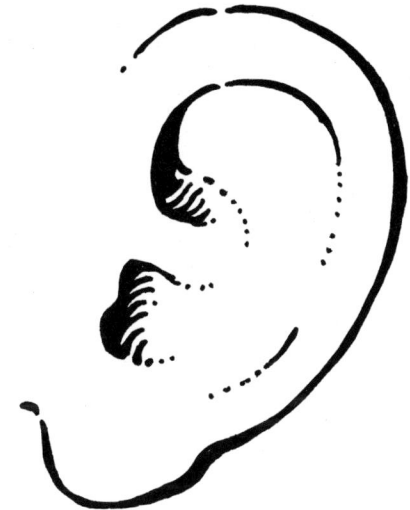
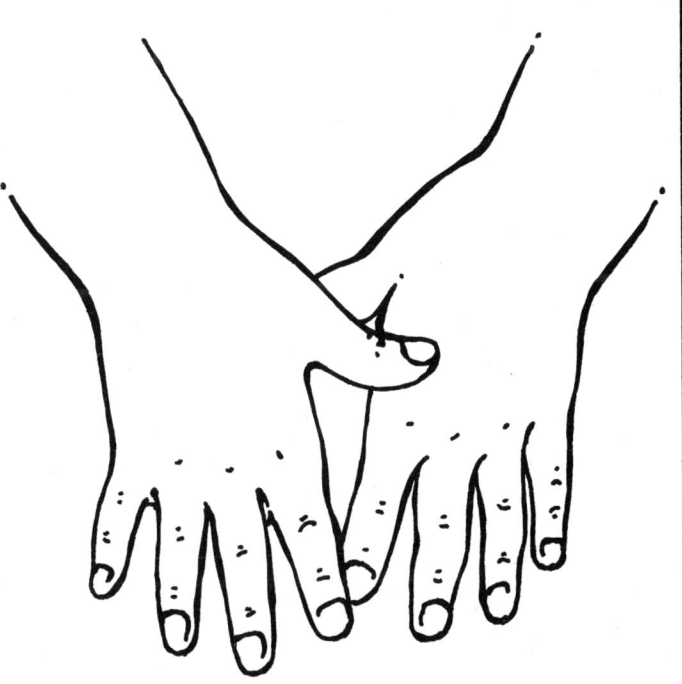
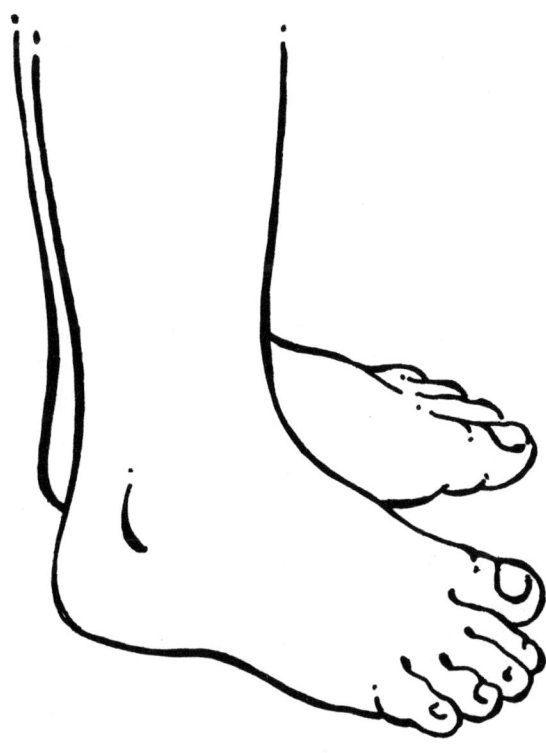

Reproducible 9B
Permission granted to photocopy for local church use. © 1998 Abingdon Press.

10 Bible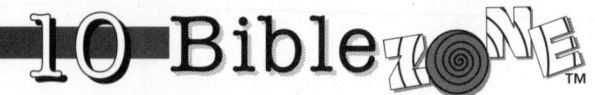

Forgive

Enter the Zone

Bible Verse
Forgive one another.
> Ephesians 4:32, *Good News Bible*

Bible Story
Matthew 18:21-22

Jesus had been telling his followers how they should act toward other believers and toward everyone in the world. As so often happened, Peter, acting as spokesperson for the disciples, came to him with a question. Peter wanted Jesus to rule on the number of times one must forgive a person who has committed a wrong.

In the pre-Israelite period vengeance toward one who had done wrong had no limits. Among the Jewish people of Jesus' day, the number of times one forgave varied, three being the fixed number at one place, and seven in another. Peter, no doubt, knew both of these statements and believed himself to be most generous when he offered to forgive seven times.

But Jesus said that wasn't enough. Since God's mercy toward us has no limits, so our forgiveness toward others also must be limitless. Seventy-seven means that our mercy toward others must have no end.

Preschoolers are just beginning to learn to get along with others. When conflicts develop between preschoolers, it may be difficult for them to find an agreeable solution for both parties. This is true for several reasons, including limited verbal abilities that make it difficult to describe feelings with words, and an egocentric orientation to the world that makes it difficult to put oneself in another's place.

Accept the developmental characteristics of the children you teach. Encourage growth by offering your children words to describe their feelings and by demonstrating your love and concern for all members of the group.

We can forgive one another.

Scope the Zone

ZONE	TIME	SUPPLIES	ZILLIES
Zoom Into the Zone			
String Along	5 minutes	Reproducible 10A, scissors, yarn, tape	none
Feelings Follies	5 minutes	none	none
BibleZone			
Time Travel	5 minutes	none	none
Sign 'n Say	5 minutes	none	none
Forgive! Forgive!	10 minutes	none	none
Bible Verse Buzz	5 minutes	Bible, BZ Bee	none
Sing!	5 minutes	cassette player	Cassette, kazoos
LifeZone			
Scripture Picture	15 minutes	Reproducibles 10A and 10B, scissors, glue	none
Circle 'n Sign	5 minutes	none	none
Smile! Jesus Loves . . .	10 minutes	Reproducible 9A and scissors or index cards; marker; cassette player	Cassette, "Smile! Jesus loves you!" tote

Zillies™ are found in the **BibleZone™ FUNspirational™ Kit.**

PRESCHOOL 6

Zoom Into the Zone

Choose one or more activities to catch your children's interest.

Supplies:
Reproducible 10A, scissors, yarn, tape

Zillies™:
none

String Along

Photocopy the oval-shaped picture of Jesus, the triangle, and the sign language picture shapes for the words *forgive one another* **(Reproducible 10A)** for each child. Cut out the shapes. Save the triangle and the sign language pictures to use later in the lesson.

Cut yarn into long lengths for each child. Tape one end of the yarn onto the Jesus picture. Hide the pictures in your room and weave the remaining lengths of yarn throughout the room. Go over, under, and around table legs, chairs, toys, blocks, and so forth. Give each child one of the loose ends of yarn.

Say: Today our Bible verse is something someone special taught us to do. Follow the yarn to find out who the special person was.

Have the child follow the yarn to find the picture of Jesus.

Ask: Who was the special person? *(Jesus)*

Say: Jesus taught us to forgive one another.

We can forgive one another.

Supplies:
none

Zillies™:
none

Feelings Follies

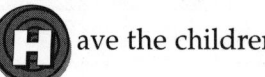**H**ave the children stand in a circle.

Say: Jesus taught us to forgive one another. How do you think it feels to forgive someone? *(Let the children respond.)* **I think forgiving someone feels like a smile. Let's send smiles around our circle.**

Turn to one of the children next to you. Smile at the child. Have that child turn to the next child and smile. Continue around the circle.

Continue the game with other statements and motions.

I think forgiving someone feels like: a handshake *(shake hands around the circle);* **a pat on the back** *(pat around the circle);* **a hug** *(hug around the circle).*

BibleZone™

Bible

Choose one or more activities to immerse your children in the Bible story.

Time Travel

Supplies: none

Zillies™: none

Use the following movement activity to lead the children to the story area. Repeat until you are ready to stop in the story area. Then end with verse 2.

Verse 1:
It's time to hear our story today.
Follow me and do what I say.
Let's walk!
(Walk around the room.)
Let's hop!
(Hop around the room.)
Let's march!
(March around the room.)

Verse 2:
Let's stop!
(Stand still.)
Look up. Look down.
(Look up; look down.)
Now turn around.
(Turn around.)
Sit down!
(Sit down.)

Sign 'n Say

Supplies: none

Zillies™: none

Teach the children the Bible verse, "Forgive one another" (Ephesians 4:32, *Good News Bible*), in American Sign Language.

Forgive — Hold out the left palm. Wipe the edge of the palm with the fingertips of the right hand.

one another — Make fists with both hands, thumbs pointing out. Hold the left hand with the thumb facing up. Hold the right hand with the thumb facing down. Circle both thumbs counterclockwise around each other.

Bible Zone Story

Forgive! Forgive!

by Lorri Coates and Barbara McKone

ave the children stand in a circle in your story area. Tell the children the story and do the motions for the cheer. Accent the words or syllables in darker type.

A disciple named Peter once went to Jesus to ask a question. "How many times am I suppose to forgive people who treated others badly?" Peter asked. "Should I forgive seven times?" What do you think Jesus' answer was?

"Seventy-seven," Jesus answered.

Seventy-seven! That's a lot! What Jesus meant is that God wants us to always forgive, no matter how many times someone treats us badly.

Let's learn something fun to help us remember that God wants us to always forgive. Everyone, stand up and get ready! *(Demonstrate the cheer for the children. Have the children repeat the cheer and motions with you. Accent the words or syllables in darker type.)*

I **want** to **live** like **Je**-sus **lived!**
For-**give!** *(Clap, clap.)*
For-**give!** *(Stomp, stomp.)*

Good job! Now, let's try out what we've learned. Let's think. What should we do if our sister or brother doesn't want to play with us, and our feelings get hurt? Let's try out our cheer.

I **want** to **live** like **Je**-sus **lived!**
For-**give!** *(Clap, clap.)*
For-**give!** *(Stomp, stomp.)*

What if we are at preschool, and a friend says something mean about a picture we've drawn?

I **want** to **live** like **Je**-sus **lived!**
For-**give!** *(Clap, clap.)*
For-**give!** *(Stomp, stomp.)*

Can you think of any other times when we should forgive? *(Allow the children to offer situations when they needed to forgive someone. Do the cheer after each example.)*

I **want** to **live** like **Je**-sus **lived!**
For-**give!** *(Clap, clap.)*
For-**give!** *(Stomp, stomp.)*

Zone In With BZ Bee

Bible Verse Buzz

Choose a child to hold the Bible open to Ephesians 4:32.

Say: Today our Bible story tells us that Jesus said to forgive one another.

Say the Bible verse, "Forgive one another" (Ephesians 4:32, *Good News Bible*), for the children. Have the children say the Bible verse after you.

Turn your back to the children or hide your hands underneath a table or behind the **BibleZone™ FUNspirational™ Kit** lid as you place the **BZ Bee puppet** (see page 174) on your hand. Turn around or bring the puppet out where the children can see it.

Pretend to make the puppet talk. Change your voice for the puppet:

Bzzz. Bzzz. Bzzz. Hi, everybody! I'm BZ Bee. *Bzzz. Bzzz. Bzzz.* I like to taste fingers. Do you have fingers? Yum, yum, yum. Let me taste.

Go to each child. Encourage, but do not force, each child to hold up his or her fingers. Have BZ pretend to taste each child's fingers. Have BZ say things like:

Mmmm. Mmmm. You taste like honey.
Bzzz. Bzzz. You taste like strawberries.
Yumm. Yumm. You taste like blueberries.

After BZ has tasted each child's fingers, say:

Bzzz. Bzzz. Bzzz. I like to taste your fingers. They're yummy. (*Rub BZ's stomach.*)

Bzzz. Bzzz. Bzzz. I like something else even more than fingers.

I like the Bible. *Bzzz. Bzzz. Bzzz.* You heard a Bible story today. Who taught Peter in our Bible story? (*Jesus*) What did Jesus tell Peter and his friends? (*to forgive one another*)

Bzzz. Bzzz. Bzzz. Jesus taught his friends to forgive one another.

 **We can forgive one another.**

Bzzz. Bzzz. Bzzz. Let's say the Bible verse together.

"Forgive one another" (Ephesians 4:32, *Good News Bible*).

Have the children repeat the Bible verse with BZ Bee.

Have BZ Bee say good-bye to the children. Put the puppet away.

Bible

Choose one or more activities to immerse your children in the Bible story.

Supplies:
cassette player

Zillies™:
Cassette, kazoos

Sing!

Say: Today our Bible story is about something Jesus taught his friends. One of the things Jesus taught is that we should forgive one another. When we forgive one another, we are being nice.

Give each child a **kazoo**. Play the song "Be Nice" from the **Cassette**. Let the children play their kazoos with the music.

NOTE: Wash the kazoos in soap and water before using them again.

Be Nice

When someone is mean to you
There's only one thing you should do,
This is my advice (What is it?)
Be nice. (Be nice?)
Be nice, be nice, be nice.

'Cause it's nice to be nice in all you do,
Not just when someone's nice to you.
If somebody calls you names,
Don't go out and do the same,
Remember this advice: (What is it?)
Be nice. (Be nice?)
Be nice, be nice, be nice, be nice, be nice.

When somebody bursts your bubble,
Better not start makin' trouble,
This is my advice: (What is it?)
Be nice.
Be nice,
Be nice, be nice, be nice.

Writers: Janet McMahan-Wilson and Debra Black
© 1991 New Spring Publishing, Inc. (ASCAP) (a div. of Brentwood-Benson Music Publishing, Inc.)
All rights reserved. Used by permission.

From the Brentwood Music, Inc. recording *God's Way A Song A Day vol. 1*.

Choose one or more activities to bring the Bible to life.

Scripture Picture

Supplies:
Reproducibles 10A and 10B, scissors, glue

Zillies™:
none

(P) hotocopy the oval-shaped picture of Jesus, the triangle, and the sign language picture shapes for the words *forgive one another* **(Reproducible 10A)** for each child. Cut out the shapes. Photocopy the shape outline page **(Reproducible 10B)**. Do not cut out these shapes. Give each child the shape outline page. Place all the shape cutout pictures on the table.

Say: Our Bible verse for today is "Forgive one another" (Ephesians 4:32, *Good News Bible*). Let's make a shape picture that shows us our Bible verse. Who told us to forgive one another? *(Jesus)* **Find the oval picture of Jesus.**

Let the children look through the pictures on the table. Help each child find an oval picture of Jesus.

Say: This picture is shaped like an egg. It is an oval. Find the matching shape on your paper, then glue your picture of Jesus on top of the matching shape.

Let the children glue the pictures of Jesus onto the matching ovals on their shape pages. Do not be concerned if the children glue their pictures in other places on their pages.

Help each child find a triangle with the words *wants us to*.

Say: Jesus wants us to forgive one another. The words in the triangle say "wants us to." Glue the triangle on top of the triangle on your shape page.

Let the children glue the triangle shapes onto the matching triangles on their shape pages.

Ask: What does Jesus want us to do? Jesus wants us to forgive one another. Find the circle shape that shows the sign for the word *forgive*. *(Sign the word for the children.)*

Help each child find a circle picture of the sign for *forgive*. Let the children glue the circles onto the matching circles on their shape pages.

Say: Find the square shape that shows the sign for the words *one another*. (Sign the word for the children.)

Help each child find a square picture of the sign for *one another*. Let the children glue the squares onto the matching squares on their shape pages. Say the Scripture picture with the children, pointing to each picture as you **say: Jesus wants us to forgive one another.**

PRESCHOOL 6

125

Life Zone

Choose one or more activities to bring the Bible to life.

Supplies:
none

Zillies™:
none

Circle 'n Sign

Have the children stand in a circle. Sing the song printed below to the tune of "London Bridge." Do the motions with the children.

Jesus wants us to forgive,
(Walk around the circle.)
To forgive, to forgive.
Jesus wants us to forgive.
Forgive one another.
(Stop walking: sign "Forgive one another.")

Supplies:
Reproducible 9A and scissors; or index cards; marker; cassette player

Zillies™:
Cassette, "Smile! Jesus loves you!" tote

Smile! Jesus Loves ...

Photocopy and cut apart the smile heart on page 116 **(Reproducible 9A)** for each child. Or use index cards. Write each child's name in large block letters on the hearts or cards. Place all the cards inside the **"Smile! Jesus loves you!" tote.** Have the children sit in a circle on the floor. Show the children the tote.

Say: Today we learned that Jesus wants us to forgive.

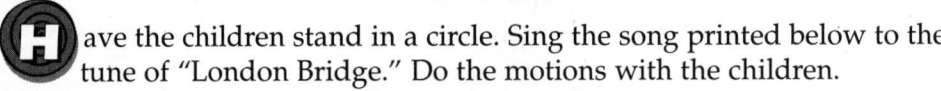

We can forgive one another.

Say: Jesus was a special teacher. He taught us about God and God's love. We know that Jesus loves each one of us.

Pass the tote around the circle. Play music from the **Cassette** or sing "Jesus Loves Me." Stop the music. Have the child holding the tote reach in and pull out a name card. Say the name printed on the card. Have that child stand up.

Say: *(Child's name)*, Jesus loves you. Thank you, God, for Jesus and for *(child's name)*. Amen.

Repeat the game until every name has been drawn from the tote and you have prayed for every child.

Photocopy the **HomeZone™** newsletter to send home to parents.

Home Zone For Parents

Bible Verse
Forgive one another.
Ephesians 4:32,
Good News Bible

Bible Story
Matthew 18:21-22

Forgive

Today your child heard that Jesus taught about forgiveness. Jesus had been telling his followers how they should act toward other believers and toward those in the world. Peter came to Jesus with a question. Peter wanted to know how many times he was required to forgive a person who has committed a wrong. He asked Jesus if he should forgive someone seven times.

Jesus said no, not seven times, but seventy-seven. What Jesus meant is that God wants us to always forgive, no matter how many times someone treats us badly. As God's mercy toward us has no limits, so our forgiveness toward others also must be limitless.

Preschoolers are just beginning to learn to get along with others. When conflicts develop between preschoolers, it may be difficult for them to find an agreeable solution for both parties because of limited language skills that make it difficult to describe feelings with words. Encourage growth in your child by offering words to describe his or her feelings. Help your child understand that other people have those same feelings.

Sign and Say

Say the Bible verse, "Forgive one another" (Ephesians 4:32, *Good News Bible*), in American Sign Language with your child.

Forgive — Hold out the left palm. Wipe the edge of the palm with the fingertips of the right hand.

one another — Make fists with both hands, thumbs pointing out. Hold the left hand with the thumb facing up. Hold the right hand with the thumb facing down. Circle both thumbs counterclockwise around each other.

We can forgive one another.

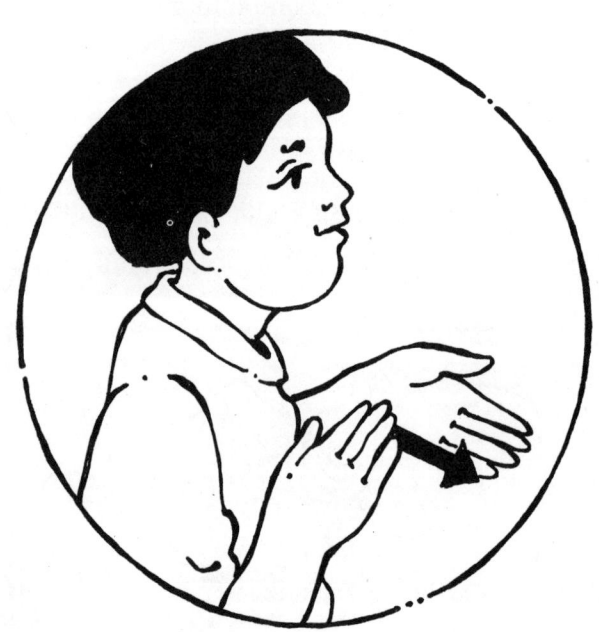

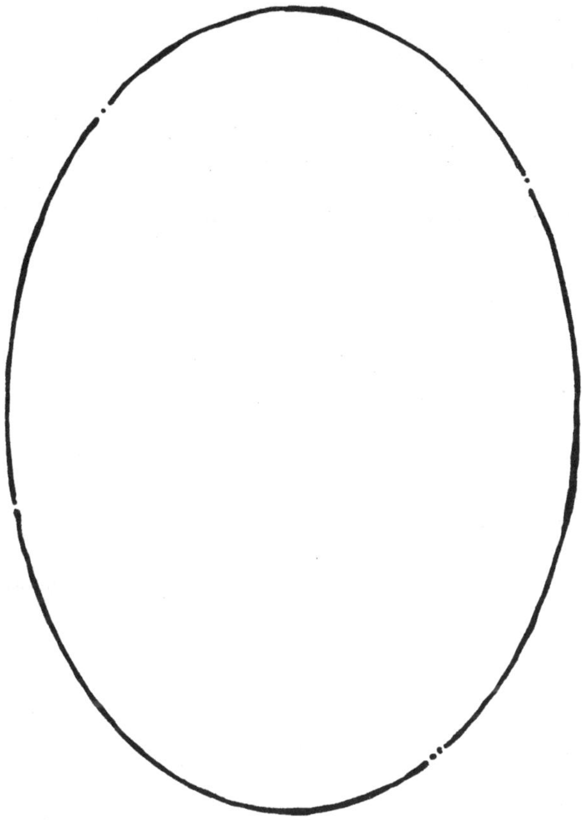

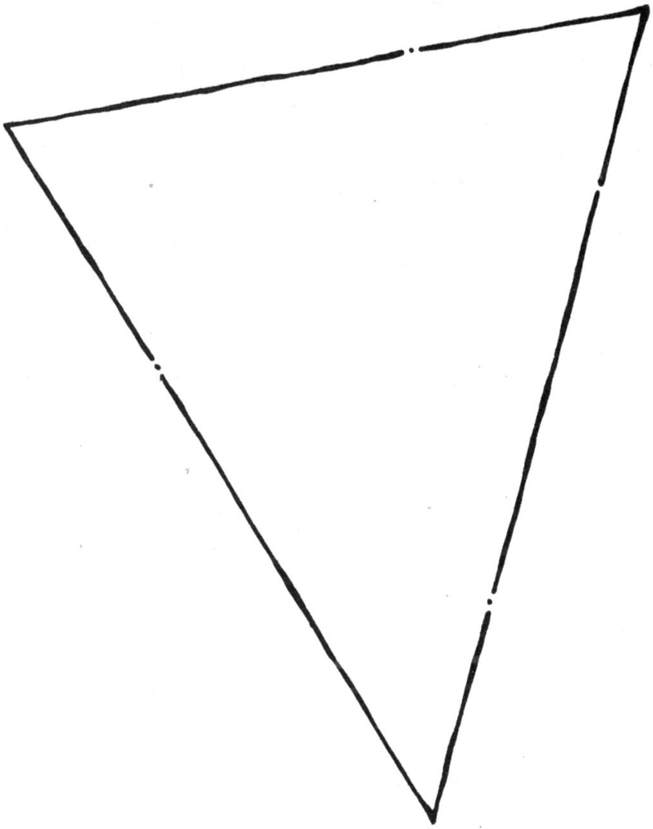

Jesus

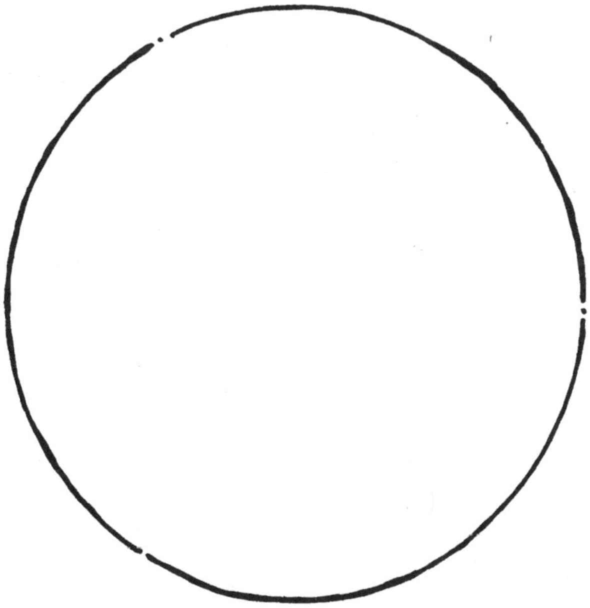

forgive one another.
Ephesians 4:32, *Good News Bible*

PRESCHOOL 6 **Reproducible 10B**
Permission granted to photocopy for local church use. © 1998 Abingdon Press.

11 Bible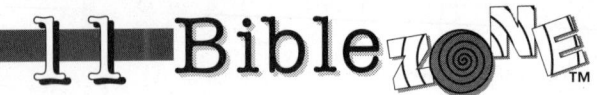

The Least of These

Enter the Zone

Bible Verse
Be kind to one another.
Ephesians 4:32

Bible Story
Matthew 25:31-40

The parable for today's lesson is often referred to as the Judgment of the Nations or the Parable of the Last Judgment. This story captures the spirit of what it means to be a follower of Christ. It preserves a theme that is found throughout the Gospels—the decisions we make now in relation to Jesus determine our destiny for eternity.

In this final judgment all the nations are judged, not just Israel. They are separated into the sheep and the goats. The sheep are those worthy to enter the kingdom; the goats are those who are not. The decision is made based on acts of mercy performed for the less fortunate. It is not how righteous a person appears to be, but how a person lives out the faith that is important. A surprising element is that those who are welcomed into the kingdom have no consciousness of their actions.

According to Jesus, God expects us to minister to the needs of others. When we love God, ministering to others is a response to that love. God wants action—not words.

The concrete images of this parable were not lost on Jesus' audience. In Bible lands, herds of sheep and goats would have been separated by the shepherd. The right hand was also the side of honor and blessing. Jesus was subtly letting the people know that God was not fooled by false appearances and would have no trouble recognizing who was a true child of God.

Sharing is an important and constantly developing part of the lives of young children. Stories about sharing with others, and your own personal examples of sharing, are important teaching tools for your children. Just as important to their development is their discovering that making choices carries consequences, whether the choice involves sharing with friends or siblings or someone else.

Always remind your children that sharing with one another is important. Be sure to commend your children for acts of sharing that you observe while they are in your care. Remind your children that when they love God, their love for God automatically shows up in love for others.

We can help others.

Scope the Zone

ZONE	TIME	SUPPLIES	ZILLIES™
Zoom Into the Zone			
Baa, Baa, Bandanna	15 minutes	Reproducible 11A, crayons or markers, tape	bandanna
Sheep, Sheep, Goat	5 minutes	none	none
BibleZone™			
Time Travel	5 minutes	none	none
Sign 'n Say	5 minutes	none	none
Sheep or Goat?	10 minutes	Reproducibles 11A and 11B	none
Bible Verse Buzz	5 minutes	Bible, BZ Bee	none
Sing!	5 minutes	cassette player	Cassette
LifeZone			
Sheep Shenanigans	10 minutes	none	none
Finger Friends	5 minutes	none	finger puppets
Circle 'n Sign	5 minutes	none	none
Smile! Jesus Loves . . .	10 minutes	Reproducible 9A and scissors; or index cards; marker; cassette player	Cassette, "Smile! Jesus loves you!" tote

Zillies™ are found in the **BibleZone™ FUNspirational™ Kit.**

Zoom Into the Zone

Choose one or more activities to catch your children's interest.

Supplies:
Reproducible 11A, crayons or markers, tape

Zillies™:
bandanna

Baa, Baa, Bandanna

Photocopy the sheep pictures **(Reproducible 11A)** for each child. Give each child a sheep picture. Let the children decorate their pictures with crayons or markers.

Say: Today we will hear about a story Jesus told his friends. In the story Jesus said that people were like sheep and goats. Jesus said that people who were like sheep were kind to one another. One way we can be kind to one another is to help others.

We can help others.

Tape each child's picture to the child's back. Have the children sit down on the floor.

Say: Let's pretend to be sheep. Let me hear you *baa* like a sheep. Very good. Let's play a game. I am going to throw this bandanna up in the air. While the bandanna is falling down, *baa* like a sheep as loud as you can. When the bandanna touches the floor, stop *baa*ing and be very quiet. Remember, stop *baa*ing as soon as the bandanna hits the floor.

Throw the **bandanna** up in the air. Encourage the children to *baa* like a sheep as long as the bandanna is falling. Have the children stop when the bandanna touches the ground.

Supplies:
none

Zillies™:
none

Sheep, Sheep, Goat

Have the children sit in a circle on the floor to play a game like "Duck, Duck, Goose."

Say: Today our Bible story is about a story Jesus told his friends. In the story Jesus said that people were like sheep and goats.

Choose a child to be the tapper. Have the tapper walk around the outside of the circle, tap each child on the head, and say, "Sheep." Then have the child tap one child on the head and say, "Goat." The "goat" jumps up and chases the tapper around the circle until the tapper sits down in the vacant space. The runner becomes the new tapper.

Bible Zone

Choose one or more activities to immerse your children in the Bible story.

Time Travel

Supplies: none

Zillies™: none

Use the following movement activity to lead the children to the story area. Repeat until you are ready to stop in the story area. Then end with verse 2.

Verse 1:
It's time to hear our story today.
Follow me and do what I say.
Let's walk!
(Walk around the room.)
Let's hop!
(Hop around the room.)
Let's march!
(March around the room.)

Verse 2:
Let's stop!
(Stand still.)
Look up. Look down.
(Look up; look down.)
Now turn around.
(Turn around.)
Sit down!
(Sit down.)

Sign 'n Say

Supplies: none

Zillies™: none

Teach the children the Bible verse, "Be kind to one another" (Ephesians 4:32), in American Sign Language.

Kind — Hold the left hand with the palm facing the body. Place the right palm over the heart. Then move the right hand as if winding a bandage around the left hand.

one another — Make fists with both hands, thumbs pointing out. Hold the left hand with the thumb facing up. Hold the right hand with the thumb facing down. Circle both thumbs counterclockwise around each other.

PRESCHOOL 6

133

Bible Story

Sheep or Goat?

by Lorri Coates and Barbara McKone

*Photocopy one sheep picture **(Reproducible 11A)** and one goat picture **(Reproducible 11B)**. Have the children sit down in your story area. Tell the children the story. Hold up the sheep picture when the children are to make sheep sounds. Hold up the goat picture when the children are to make goat horns.*

Once Jesus told a story to explain how we should treat one another. In his story Jesus said that people were like sheep and goats.

Jesus said that people who act like sheep care about other people the way Jesus cared for everyone. They were kind to one another. People who acted like sheep would give food to someone who was hungry *(pretend to eat);* give a drink to someone who was thirsty *(pretend to drink);* make a visitor feel welcome *(shake hands);* take care of someone who was sick *(put hand on forehead);* and visit people who were sick or in prison *(cross fists at wrists).*

Let's make a sound like a sheep. *Baa, Baa.* *(Hold up sheep picture. Have the children **baa**.)*

Jesus said that people who acted like goats thought some people weren't important enough to care about. A goat wouldn't help someone who needed help. They were not *(shake head no)* kind to one another. People who acted like goats would not *(shake head no)* give food to someone who was hungry *(pretend to eat);* they would not *(shake head no)* give a drink to someone who was thirsty *(pretend to drink);* they would not *(shake head no)* make a visitor feel welcome *(shake hands);* they would not *(shake head no)* take care of someone who was sick *(put hand on forehead);* and they would not *(shake head no)* visit people who were sick or in prison *(cross fists at wrists).*

Let's make goat horns. Put your pointer fingers up on your head to make horns. *(Hold up goat picture. Have the children use their index fingers to make goat horns.)*

Now I am going to tell you some stories about people, and you let me know whether they are acting like sheep or goats. If they are acting like sheep, you say, "Baa, baa!" If they are acting like goats, put your goat horns on top of your head. Here we go!

Natasha sees a new girl coming into Sunday school. Natasha decides to play with the new girl. Is Natasha acting like a sheep or a goat? *(Hold up sheep picture. Have the children **baa**.)*

Michael and his family take food to the homeless shelter every month. Is Michael acting like a sheep or a goat? *(Hold up sheep picture. Have the children **baa**.)*

A man is driving home from work and sees a boy fall off his bike. The boy is lying on the sidewalk crying because he has been hurt. The man drives on past the boy without trying to help. Is the man acting like a sheep or a goat? *(Hold up goat picture. Have the children make goat horns.)*

Jesus said that when we acted like sheep and helped someone, it would be like helping him. Let's all be sheep. *(Hold up sheep picture. Have the children **baa**.)*

Zone In With BZ Bee

Bible Verse Buzz

hoose a child to hold the Bible open to Ephesians 4:32.

Say: Jesus told his friends a story. In the story Jesus said that people were like sheep and goats. Jesus said that people who were like sheep were kind to one another.

Say the Bible verse, "Be kind to one another" (Ephesians 4:32), for the children. Have the children say the Bible verse after you.

Turn your back to the children or hide your hands underneath a table or behind the **BibleZone™ FUNspirational™ Kit** lid as you place the **BZ Bee puppet** (see page 174) on your hand. Turn around or bring the puppet out where the children can see it.

Pretend to make the puppet talk. Change your voice for the puppet:

Bzzz. Bzzz. Bzzz. Hi, everybody! I'm BZ Bee. *Bzzz. Bzzz. Bzzz.* I like to taste fingers. Do you have fingers? Yum, yum, yum. Let me taste.

Go to each child. Encourage, but do not force, each child to hold up his or her fingers. Have BZ pretend to taste each child's fingers. Have BZ say things like:

Mmmm. Mmmm. You taste like honey.
Bzzz. Bzzz. You taste like strawberries.
Yumm. Yumm. You taste like blueberries.

After BZ has tasted each child's fingers, say:

Bzzz. Bzzz. Bzzz. I like to taste your fingers. They're yummy. (*Rub BZ's stomach.*)

Bzzz. Bzzz. Bzzz. I like something else even more than fingers.

I like the Bible. *Bzzz. Bzzz. Bzzz.* Today you heard a story Jesus told his friends. Jesus said that people were like what two animals? (*sheep and goats*)

Bzzz. Bzzz. Bzzz. In the story Jesus said that people were like sheep and goats. Jesus said that people who were like sheep were kind to one another. One way we can be kind to one another is to help others.

 **We can help others.**

Bzzz. Bzzz. Bzzz. Let's say the Bible verse together.

"Be kind to one another" (Ephesians 4:32).

Have the children repeat the Bible verse with BZ Bee.

Have BZ Bee say good-bye to the children. Put the puppet away.

Bible

Choose one or more activities to immerse your children in the Bible story.

Supplies:
cassette player

Zillies™:
Cassette

Sing!

Say: **Today we listened to a story Jesus told his friends. In the story Jesus said that people were like sheep and goats. Jesus said that people who were like sheep were kind to one another. One way we can be kind to one another is to help others. Let's listen to a song that tells us about helping others.**

Have the children stand in a circle. Play the song "The Blessing" from the **Cassette.** Do the suggested circle dance with the children as the music plays.

The Blessing

(Hold hands. Walk around the circle.)
Bless you, my child, for you have been a blessing.
May the good Lord smile down upon you this day,
for you gave me kindness when I was in need.
God bless you, my child, as you have blessed me.

(Walk around the circle in the opposite direction.)
Bless you, my child, for you have been a blessing.
May the good Lord smile down upon you this day,
for you gave her kindness when she was in need.
God bless you, my child, as you have blessed me.

(Walk around the circle in the opposite direction.)
Bless you, my child, for you have been a blessing.
May the good Lord smile down upon you this day,
for you gave me kindness when I was in need.
God bless you, my child, as you have blessed me.

(Drop hands. Turn around in place.)
You shared a part of you, the heart of who you are.
You did not know me, yet you showed me love.

(Hold hands. Walk around the circle.)
Bless you, my child, for you have been a blessing.
May the good Lord smile down upon you this day.
For you gave them kindness when they were in need.
God bless you, my child, as you have blessed me.
God bless you, my child, as you have blessed me.

Writers: Ted Wilson and Janet McMahan-Wilson
© 1989 New Spring Publishing, Inc. (ASCAP) and Bridge Buidling Music, Inc. (BMI) (divisions of Brentwood-Benson Music Publishing, Inc.) All rights reserved. Used by permission.

From the Brentwood-Benson Music Publishing, Inc. recording *Something's Up Down In Bethlehem.*

Life Zone

Choose one or more activities to bring the Bible to life.

Sheep Shenanigans

Supplies: none

Zillies™: none

Have the children move to the side of the room opposite your story area. Choose the children one at a time. Tell each child how to move across the room to the story area. Have the children sit down in your story area.

Say: **Jesus told his friends a story. In the story Jesus said that people were like sheep and goats. Jesus said that people who were like sheep were kind to one another. One way we can be kind to one another is to help others. We can be like sheep.**

Zone In: We can help others.

Say: **Sheep (Child's name), crawl across the room.** (Vary the movements: hop, tiptoe, jump, take giant steps, take baby steps, gallop, and so forth.)

Finger Friends

Supplies: none

Zillies™: finger puppets

Encourage the children to suggests ways we can show kindness and help others (share toys, share food, pick up toys, play quietly when someone is sick, make a get-well card or draw a picture for someone who is sick, and so forth).

Show the children the four **finger puppets** and say the following fingerplay.

> Four happy children were standing in a line.
> They all knew Jesus wants us to be kind.
> *(Hold up all four finger puppets.)*
> The first one said, "I will help someone today."
> *(Hold up first finger puppet.)*
> The second one said, "I will share toys as I play."
> *(Hold up second finger puppet.)*
> The third one said, "I will show someone I care."
> *(Hold up third finger puppet.)*
> The fourth one said, "I will bring some food to share."
> *(Hold up fourth finger puppet.)*
> Four happy children were standing in a line.
> They all knew Jesus wants us to be kind.
> *(Hold up all four finger puppets.)*

Life Zone

Choose one or more activities to bring the Bible to life.

Supplies:
none

Zillies™:
none

Circle 'n Sign

Have the children stand in a circle. Sing the song printed below to the tune of "London Bridge." Do the motions with the children. (See page 133 for sign language.)

Jesus wants us to be kind,
(Walk around the circle.)
To be kind, to be kind.
Jesus wants us to be kind.
Be kind to one another.
(Stop walking: sign "Be kind to one another.")

Supplies:
Reproducible 9A and scissors; or index cards; marker; cassette player

Zillies™:
Cassette, "Smile! Jesus loves you!" tote

Smile! Jesus Loves ...

Photocopy and cut apart the smile heart on page 116 (**Reproducible 9A**) for each child. Or use index cards. Write each child's name in large block letters on the hearts or cards. Place all the cards inside the **"Smile! Jesus loves you!" tote.** Have the children sit in a circle on the floor. Show the children the tote.

Say: Today we learned that Jesus wants us to be kind and to help others.

We can help others.

Say: Jesus was a special teacher. He taught us about God and about God's love. We know that Jesus loves each one of us.

Pass the tote around the circle. Play music from the **Cassette** or sing "Jesus Loves Me." Stop the music. Have the child holding the tote reach in and pull out a name card. Say the name printed on the card. Have that child stand up.

Say: *(Child's name),* **Jesus loves you. Thank you, God, for Jesus and for** *(child's name).* **Amen.**

Repeat the game until every name has been drawn from the tote and you have prayed for every child.

Photocopy the **HomeZone™** newsletter to send home to parents.

Home Zone For Parents

The Least of These

Today your child heard about a story Jesus told his friends. In the story Jesus said that people were like sheep and goats. Jesus said that people who were like sheep were kind to one another. They ministered to the needs of others. People who were like goats did not minister to the needs of others.

God expects us to be sheep; that is, God expects us to minister to the needs of others. When we love God, ministering to others is a response to that love. God wants action—not words.

Provide opportunities for your child to help others. Let your child draw pictures or make get-well cards to send to friends who are sick. Participate in food and clothing collections. Remind your child that when we love God, our love for God automatically shows up in love for others.

Sign and Say

Say the Bible verse, "Be kind to one another" (Ephesians 4:32), in American Sign Language.

Kind — Hold the left hand with the palm facing the body. Place the right palm over the heart. Then move the right hand as if winding a bandage around the left hand.

one another — Make fists with both hands, thumbs pointing out. Hold the left hand with the thumb facing up. Hold the right hand with the thumb facing down. Circle both thumbs counterclockwise around each other.

We can help others.

Reproducible 11A
Permission granted to photocopy for local church use. © 1998 Abingdon Press.

PRESCHOOL 6 **Reproducible 11B**
Permission granted to photocopy for local church use. © 1998 Abingdon Press.

12 Bible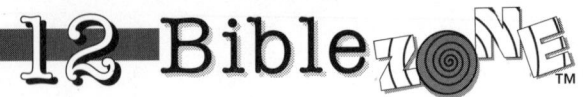

Birds of the Field

Enter the

Bible Verse
God cares for you.
1 Peter 5:7, adapted

Bible Story
Matthew 6:25-33

Here Jesus described God as the Creator and Sustainer of all life. If God cares for birds and lilies, God also will care for and provide for God's people.

The people of God, Jesus said, should not worry about food and clothing, because life is more than basic needs. Further, we cannot change our lives by worrying. Jesus was not saying that these needs are unimportant. Neither did he mean that we should not work or be diligent. Anyone who watches birds knows that they are very hard workers.

What Jesus was saying is that our concern should be first on how to fulfill what God wants. Only when we put our trust in God to care and provide for us do our anxieties about life begin to lessen. Awareness of our dependence on God frees us to focus on what God wants us to be and to do, and to strive to live in obedience to God.

Preschoolers are discovering and expanding their basic concept of God. It is important, therefore, that your teaching about God centers on the understanding that God is love. We hope that none of the children we encounter in our classrooms will know anxiety about their basic needs, but the reality is that not all children live in loving and caring environments. Their most basic needs for love and acceptance may not be being met. As a teacher of young children you are called to model God's love to all your children.

Children's self-esteem is fortified by feeling that they are important to someone. Today's lesson can help them realize how precious they are to God. The things children have, the houses they live in, and the kinds of clothes they wear are not what make them important in God's eyes.

We know God cares about each of us.

Scope the Zone

ZONE	TIME	SUPPLIES	ZILLIES™
Zoom Into the Zone			
Birds of a Feather	5 minutes	Reproducible 12A, scissors	none
Birds and Flowers	10 minutes	Reproducible 12B, crayons or markers, glue or tape	none
BibleZone™			
Time Travel	5 minutes	none	none
Sign 'n Say	5 minutes	none	none
Don't Worry	10 minutes	Reproducible 12A	none
Bible Verse Buzz	5 minutes	Bible, BZ Bee	none
Sing!	5 minutes	cassette player	Cassette
LifeZone			
Birds Fly Like This	5 minutes	none	none
Turnover Time	10 minutes	Reproducible 12A, tape, scissors	none
Circle 'n Sign	5 minutes	none	none
Smile! Jesus Loves . . .	10 minutes	Reproducible 9A and scissors, or index cards; marker; cassette player	Cassette, "Smile! Jesus loves you!" tote

Zillies™ are found in the **BibleZone™ FUNspirational™ Kit.**

PRESCHOOL 6

Zoom Into the Zone

Choose one or more activities to catch your children's interest.

Supplies:
Reproducible 12A, scissors

Zillies™:
none

Birds of a Feather

Photocopy and cut apart at least two copies of the birds and flowers pictures **(Reproducible 12A)**. Mix up the pictures and place them on a table or rug. Let the children enjoy matching the pictures.

Say: **Today we will hear a story Jesus told about how God loves and cares for us. Jesus told his friends that God cares about the birds and flowers. Then Jesus told his friends that God cares even more about people.**

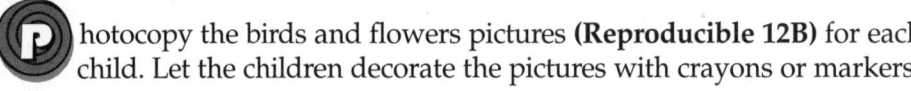

We know God cares about each of us.

Supplies:
Reproducible 12B, crayons or markers, glue or tape

Zillies™:
none

Birds and Flowers

Photocopy the birds and flowers pictures **(Reproducible 12B)** for each child. Let the children decorate the pictures with crayons or markers.

Help each child fold the page along the dotted line. Glue or tape the sides of each page together, leaving the bottom open. Show each child how to place a hand inside the bottom to make a turnaround puppet.

Say: **Today we will hear a story Jesus told about how God loves and cares for us. Jesus told his friends that God cares about the birds and flowers. Then Jesus told his friends that God cares even more about people.**

Sing the song printed below to the tune of "Twinkle, Twinkle, Little Star." Have the children hold up the bird sides of their puppets when you sing the verse about birds. Have the children turn their puppets to their flower sides when you sing about flowers.

Birdies, birdies, everywhere,
Tell us of God's love and care.
See them high up in the sky,
Ducks and redbirds flying by.
Birdies, birdies, everywhere,
Tell us of God's love and care.

Flowers, flowers, everywhere,
Tell us of God's love and care.
Growing in their flower beds,
Blue and yellow, orange and red.
Flowers, flowers, everywhere,
Tell us of God's love and care.

Bible Zone

Choose one or more activities to immerse your children in the Bible story.

Time Travel

Use the following movement activity to lead the children to the story area. Repeat the verse until you are ready to stop in the story area. Then end with verse 2.

Verse 1:
It's time to hear our story today.
Follow me and do what I say.
Let's walk!
(Walk around the room.)
Let's hop!
(Hop around the room.)
Let's march!
(March around the room.)

Verse 2:
Let's stop!
(Stand still.)
Look up. Look down.
(Look up; look down.)
Now turn around.
(Turn around.)
Sit down!
(Sit down.)

Supplies:
none

Zillies™:
none

Sign 'n Say

Teach the children the Bible verse, "God cares for you" (1 Peter 5:7, adapted) in American Sign Language.

God — Point index finger of your right hand, with the other fingers curled down. Bring the hand down and open the palm.

Cares — Hold your thumbs in front of your open palms. Alternate moving palms from the forehead level down.

You — Point out with your index finger.

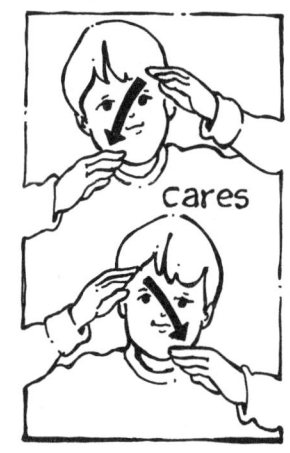

© 1998 Abingdon Press.

Supplies:
none

Zillies™:
none

Bible Zone Story

Don't Worry

by Lorri Coates and Barbara McKone

Have the children bring their birds and flowers puppets *(Reproducible 12A)* and sit down in your story area. Have the children place their puppets on the floor beside them. Encourage the children to hold up the bird sides of the puppets when you say, "Look at the birds." Encourage the children hold up the flower sides of the puppets when you say, "Look at the flowers."

Worry, worry, worry. Do you ever worry about anything? What kinds of things do you worry about? *(Give the children some time to share, but be careful to gently stop children from sharing very private things in the whole group. Give children with serious problems some individual attention after the story so that they can talk to you privately about important matters.)*

Jesus said, "Don't worry! Don't worry about your life. Don't worry about what you will eat. *(Pretend to eat.)* Don't worry about what you will drink. *(Pretend to drink.)* Don't worry about what you will wear. *(Sweep hands down to indicate clothing.)* There are more important things in life than food and clothes."

Jesus told the people not to worry about what they would wear. "Look at the birds," Jesus said. *(Hold up bird sides of puppets.)* "They don't plant gardens, but God makes sure that the birds have food to eat."

What do birds eat? Where do they find their food? Do you think God cares about you as much as God cares for the birds?

(Have the children show their bird puppets and repeat this verse after you.)

**Look at the birds, and you will see,
God will take care of you and me.**

Jesus told the people not to worry about what they would wear. "Look at the flowers growing in the field," Jesus said. *(Hold up flower sides of puppets.)* "They don't make clothes to wear, but they are beautiful."

How are flowers dressed? Do you think God cares about you as much as God cares about the flowers?

(Have the children show their flower puppets and repeat this verse after you.)

**Look at the flowers, and you will see,
God will take care of you and me.**

(Have the children place their puppets on the floor.)

Jesus said, "Don't worry! Don't say things like, 'What shall we eat? *(Pretend to eat.)* What shall we drink? *(Pretend to drink.)* What shall we wear?' *(Sweep hands down to indicate clothing.)* God knows that you need these things. The most important thing is to try to live the way God wants you to live. God will make sure that you have what you need to live. God will take care of you."

(Have the children hold up their flower and bird puppets and repeat this verse after you.)

**Listen to Jesus, and you will see,
God will take care of you and me.**

In With BZ Bee

Bible Verse Buzz

hoose a child to hold the Bible open to 1 Peter 5:7.

Say: Jesus told a story about how God loves and cares for us. Jesus said that God cares about the birds and flowers. Then Jesus said that God cares even more about people.

Say the Bible verse, "God cares for you" (1 Peter 5:7, adapted), for the children. Have the children say the Bible verse after you.

Turn your back to the children or hide your hands underneath a table or behind the **BibleZone™ FUNspirational™ Kit** lid as you place the **BZ Bee puppet** (see page 174) on your hand. Turn around or bring the puppet out where the children can see it.

Pretend to make the puppet talk. Change your voice for the puppet:

Bzzz. Bzzz. Bzzz. Hi, everybody! I'm BZ Bee. *Bzzz. Bzzz. Bzzz.* I like to taste fingers. Do you have fingers? Yum, yum, yum. Let me taste.

Go to each child. Encourage, but do not force, each child to hold up his or her fingers. Have BZ pretend to taste each child's fingers. Have BZ say things like:

Mmmm. Mmmm. You taste like honey.
Bzzz. Bzzz. You taste like strawberries.
Yumm. Yumm. You taste like blueberries.

After BZ has tasted each child's fingers, say:

Bzzz. Bzzz. Bzzz. I like to taste your fingers. They're yummy. (*Rub BZ's stomach.*)

Bzzz. Bzzz. Bzzz. I like something else even more than fingers.

I like the Bible. *Bzzz. Bzzz. Bzzz.* Today you heard a story Jesus told his friends. What did Jesus tell his friends not to do? (*worry*) What did Jesus say God cared about? (*birds and flowers*) Who did Jesus say God cared about more than the birds and flowers? (*people; you*)

Bzzz. Bzzz. Bzzz. In the story Jesus said that God cared about the birds and flowers. Then Jesus said that God cares even more about people.

 **We know God cares about each one of us.**

Bzzz. Bzzz. Bzzz. Let's say the Bible verse together.

"God cares for you" (1 Peter 5:7, adapted).

Have the children repeat the Bible verse with BZ Bee.

Have BZ Bee say good-bye to the children. Put the puppet away.

Bible

Choose one or more activities to immerse your children in the Bible story.

Supplies:
cassette player

Zillies™:
Cassette

Sing!

ave the children stand in a circle. Play the song "God's Gotta Lotta Love" from the **Cassette**. Do the motions as suggested.

God's Gotta Lotta Love

God's gotta lotta love to go around,
(Walk around in a circle.)
go around, go around.
God's gotta lotta love to go around,
so sing a happy sound.
(Stop; cup hands around mouth.)
la la la la la la

God's gotta lotta love to go around,
(Walk around in a circle.)
go around, go around.
God's gotta lotta love to go around,
so hum a happy sound.
(Stop; point to mouth.)
hm hm hm hm hm hm hm

God's gotta lotta love to go around,
(Walk around in a circle.)
go around, go around.
God's gotta lotta love to go around,
so whistle a happy sound.
(Stop; try to whistle.)
(whistle)

God's gotta lotta love to go around,
(Walk around in a circle.)
go around, go around.
God's gotta lotta love to go around,
so play a happy sound.
(Stop; pretend to play piano.)

God's gotta lotta love to go around,
(Walk around in a circle.)
go around, go around.
God's gotta lotta love to go around,
so shout a happy sound.
(Stop; wave hands above head.)
hip, hip, hooray, hip, hip, hooray,

God's gotta lotta love to go around,
(Walk around in a circle.)
go around, go around.
God's gotta lotta love to go around,
so sing a happy sound.
(Stop; cup hands around mouth.)

Writers: Janet McMahan-Wilson and Dennis Scott
© 1991 John T. Benson Publishing Co. (ASCAP) (a div. of Brentwood-Benson Music Publishing, Inc.)
All rights reserved. Used by permission.

From the Brentwood-Benson Music Publishing, Inc. recording *Time Out To Sing*.

Life Zone

Choose one or more activities to bring the Bible to life.

Birds Fly Like This

Supplies: none

Zillies™: none

Have the children move to an open area of the room.

Say: Jesus said that God cares about the birds and flowers. Let's pretend that we are birds:

> Birds fly like this. (*Have the children flap their arms like bird wings.*)
> Birds fly and hop like this. (*Have the children flap their arms and hop up and down at the same time.*)
> Birds fly and hop and wiggle their tail feathers like this. (*Have the children flap their arms, hop up and down, and wiggle their backsides at the same time.*)
> Birds fly and hop and wiggle their tail feathers and eat like this. (*Have the children flap their arms, hop up and down, wiggle their backsides, and nod their heads up and down as if pecking food at the same time.*)
> Birds fly and hop and wiggle their tail feathers and eat and then go to sleep like this. (*Have the children flap their arms, hop up and down, wiggle their backsides, and nod their heads up and down as if pecking food at the same time. Then have the children sit down, tuck their heads under their arms, and pretend to sleep.*)

Say: Then Jesus said that God cares even more about people. We know God cares for each one of us.

Turnover Time

Supplies: Reproducible 12A, tape, scissors

Zillies™: none

Photocopy and cut apart the birds and flowers pictures (**Reproducible 12A**). Make sure you have one picture for each child. Have the children stand in a circle. Tape a bird picture onto the clothing of the first child in the circle. Tape a flower picture onto the clothing of the second child. Continue alternating bird and flower pictures around the circle.

Play a game with the children like fruit basket turnover.

Say: Let's pretend that we are flowers and birds. When I say, "God cares for birds," everyone with a bird picture change places. When I say, "God cares for flowers," everyone with a flower picture change places. When I say, "God cares for you," everyone change places.

Help the children know when to change places. Play the game several times.

Life Zone

Choose one or more activities to bring the Bible to life.

Supplies:
none

Zillies™:
none

Circle 'n Sign

Have the children stand in a circle. Sing the song printed below to the tune of "London Bridge." Do the motions with the children.

Jesus said God cares for you,
(Walk around the circle.)
Cares for you, cares for you.
Jesus said God cares for you,
God cares for you.
(Stop walking: sign "God cares for you.")

Supplies:
Reproducible 9A and scissors; or index cards; marker; cassette player

Zillies™:
Cassette, "Smile! Jesus loves you!" tote

Smile! Jesus Loves . . .

Photocopy and cut apart the smile heart on page 116 **(Reproducible 9A)** for each child. Or use index cards. Write each child's name in large block letters on the hearts or cards. Place all the cards inside the **"Smile! Jesus loves you!" tote.** Have the children sit in a circle on the floor. Show the children the tote.

Say: Today we learned that Jesus said God loves and cares for us.

 **We know God cares about each of us.**

Say: Jesus was a special teacher. He taught us about God and God's love. We know that Jesus loves each one of us.

Pass the tote around the circle. Play music from the **Cassette** or sing "Jesus Loves Me." Stop the music. Have the child holding the tote reach in and pull out a name card. Say the name printed on the card. Have that child stand up.

Say: *(Child's name)*, Jesus loves you. Thank you, God, for Jesus and for *(child's name)*. Amen.

Repeat the game until every name has been drawn from the tote and you have prayed for every child.

Photocopy the **HomeZone™** newsletter to send home to parents.

Home Zone For Parents

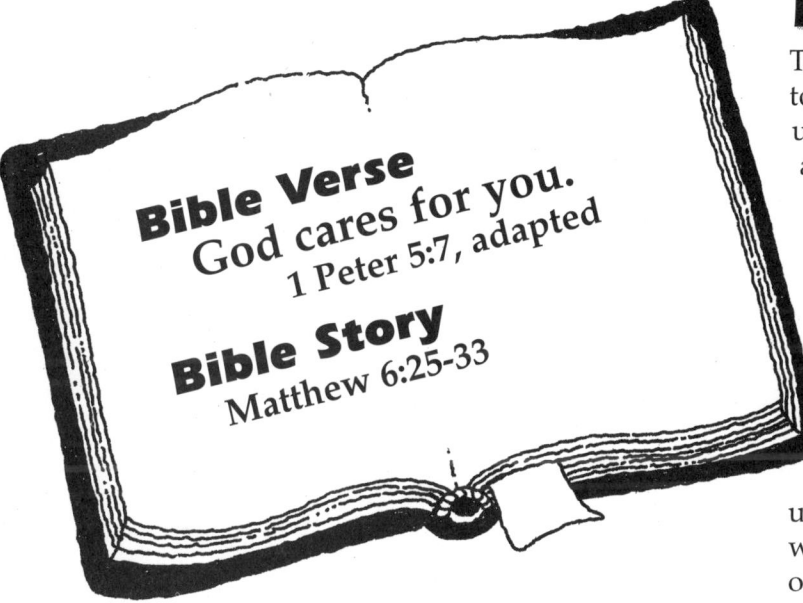

Bible Verse
God cares for you.
1 Peter 5:7, adapted

Bible Story
Matthew 6:25-33

Birds of the Field

Today your child heard a story Jesus told about how God loves and cares for us. Jesus told his friends that God cares about the birds and flowers. Then Jesus told his friends that God cares even more about people.

With this story Jesus reminds us that we should not worry about food and clothing, because life is more than basic needs. Further, we cannot change our lives by worrying. Jesus was not saying that these needs are unimportant. Neither did he mean that we should not work or be diligent. Anyone who watches birds knows that they are very hard workers.

What Jesus was saying is that our concern should be first on how to fulfill what God wants. Only when we put our trust in God to care and provide for us do our anxieties about life begin to lessen. Awareness of our dependence on God frees us to focus on what God wants us to be and to do, and to strive to live in obedience to God.

Children's self-esteem is fortified by feeling that they are important to someone. Today's lesson can help your child realize how precious she or he is to God.

Bird's Nest Cookies

Enjoy making bird's nest cookies with your child. Remind your child that God cares for the birds and that God cares even more for us.

1 cup peanut butter
1 cup nonfat dry milk
½ cup crushed corn flakes
1 teaspoon vanilla
1 cup honey
jelly beans

Mix together peanut butter, nonfat dry milk, honey, and vanilla. Roll the peanut butter mixture into small balls. Then roll the balls into crushed corn flakes and shape the balls into bird's nests. Add jelly beans for eggs.

We know God cares about each of us.

Reproducible 12A

Permission granted to photocopy for local church use. © 1998 Abingdon Press.

13 Bible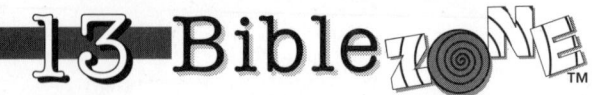

The Golden Rule

Enter the

Bible Verse
Do for others what you want them to do for you.
Matthew 7:12, Good News Bible

Bible Story
Matthew 7:12

What we know as the Golden Rule is found in one form or another not only in Judaism, but also in several other religious traditions. In the traditions of Jesus day, however, this knowledge was presented in a negative form—people were called to avoid doing to others what they would not like to have done to themselves. Jesus reinvented the Golden Rule for his followers as a summation of the commandment to love one's enemies. Jesus' challenge to us is to go beyond simply not doing wrong. As Christians we are called to go the extra mile. The Golden Rule says to us that we should think about others and their happiness.

The Golden Rule summarizes the instructions that Jesus gives for holy living. The author of Matthew explains why the Golden Rule was included, stating that it explains the law of Moses and the prophets.

Matthew's gospel seeks to connect Jesus' teaching to Jewish tradition. Jesus has restated the law, and that is why it is important to us as Christians. Without the context of holy living in which Jesus places the Golden Rule, it could be used to justify inappropriate behavior rooted in sinful human desire. This is clearly not Jesus' message. Instead, he teaches mutual respect and compassion, summarizing his teachings on right living under the law.

Young children may have difficulty applying the Golden Rule because they are unable to put themselves in another person's place. It is often difficult for them to view situations from anything other than their own perspectives. However, they can understand that they like to be treated with kindness, and they need to be taught that others have these feelings too. Learning to respect the feelings of others is an important lesson of childhood, and indeed, of life.

As a teacher of young children you can help your children learn to apply the Golden Rule in their relationships with others. Pray for guidance in knowing what God wants you to do for others and encourage your children to pray for others.

We can treat others the way we want to be treated.

Scope the Zone

ZONE	TIME	SUPPLIES	ZILLIES
Zoom Into the Zone			
Bible Verse Bracelets	10 minutes	Reproducible 13A, scissors or paper cutter, crayons or markers, tape or glue	none
Echo Echo	5 minutes	wrist bands (Reproducible 13A)	none
BibleZone			
Time Travel	5 minutes	none	none
Finger Friends	5 minutes	none	finger puppets
The Golden Rule	10 minutes	wrist bands (Reproducible 13A)	none
Bible Verse Buzz	5 minutes	Bible, BZ Bee	none
Sing!	5 minutes	cassette player	Cassette
LifeZone			
Skip, Hop, Jump	10 minutes	none	none
Golden Grams	10 minutes	Reproducible 13B, gold or yellow crayon or marker, crayons or markers	none
Circle 'n Sing	5 minutes	none	none
Smile! Jesus Loves...	5 minutes	cassette player	Cassette, "Smile! Jesus loves you!" tote

Zillies™ are found in the **BibleZone™ FUNspirational™ Kit.**

Zoom Into the Zone

Choose one or more activities to catch your children's interest.

Supplies:
Reproducible 13A, scissors or paper cutter, crayons or markers, tape or glue

Zillies™:
none

Bible Verse Bracelets

 hotocopy the wrist streamer page **(Reproducible 13A)** for each child. Use a paper cutter or scissors to cut apart the wrist band and streamers. Give each child a wrist band (the Bible verse is printed on the wrist band). Let the children decorate the wrist bands with crayons or markers.

Say: Today our Bible story is about an important rule Jesus taught his friends. We call the rule the Golden Rule. The rule tells us how God wants us to live. This is the rule: "Do for others what you want them to do for you" (Matthew 7:12, *Good News Bible*). That means if we want other people to be kind to us, we should be kind to them.

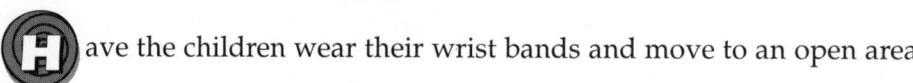

We can treat others the way we want to be treated.

Help each child roll the wrist band into a tube large enough to slip over the child's wrist. Tape the sides of the tubes together. Give each child the streamers. Help the children glue or tape the streamers around the wrist band. Encourage the children to wear the wrist bands to your story area.

Supplies:
wrist bands (Reproducible 13A)

Zillies™:
none

Echo Echo

Have the children wear their wrist bands and move to an open area.

Say: Let's pretend that you are my echo. When I say and do something. You say and do it just exactly like I do.

Say the following words and do the motions as suggested. Encourage the children to repeat the words and motions to you.

I'm so-o-o glad you're here. *(Speak in a happy tone; wave wrist band excitedly.)*
You're not my friend! *(Shout in an angry tone; put hands on hips.)*
I like you! *(Shout in a happy tone: throw arms up in the air.)*

Say: How did you feel when I said "I like you?" How did you feel when I said "You're not my friend?" Today our Bible story is about an important rule Jesus taught his friends. The rule tells us to treat others the way we want to be treated. If we want others to be kind to us, we should be kind to them.

BibleZone™

Bible

Choose one or more activities to immerse your children in the Bible story.

Time Travel

Supplies: none

Zillies™: none

Use the following movement activity to lead the children to the story area. Repeat the verse until ready to stop in story area Then end with verse 2.

Verse 1:
It's time to hear our story today.
Follow me and do what I say.
Let's walk!
(Walk around the room.)
Let's hop!
(Hop around the room.)
Let's march!
(March around the room.)

Verse 2:
Let's stop!
(Stand still.)
Look up. Look down.
(Look up; look down.)
Now turn around.
(Turn around.)
Sit down!
(Sit down.)

Finger Friends

Supplies: none

Zillies™: finger puppets

Say: Today our Bible story is about an important rule Jesus taught his friends. The rule tells us to treat others the way we want to be treated. How do you like to be treated? Encourage the children to suggest ways they like to be treated (*good, nicely, like a friend, and so forth*).

Show the children the **four finger puppets** and say the following fingerplay:

Four happy children came to their church school.
They all knew Jesus taught a special rule.
(Hold up all four finger puppets.)
The first one said, "I'll remember to be kind."
(Hold up first finger puppet.)
The second one said, "A new friend I will find."
(Hold up second finger puppet.)
The third one said, "I'll wait my turn to play."
(Hold up third finger puppet.)
The fourth one said, "I'll share my toys today."
(Hold up fourth finger puppet.)
Four happy children came to their church school.
They all knew Jesus taught the Golden rule.
(Hold up all four finger puppets.)

Bible Zone Story

The Golden Rule

by Lorri Coates and Barbara McKone

ave the children wear their wrist bands and sit down in your story area. Tell the children the story. Have the children wave their wrist bands high in the air as suggested.

God always wants us to treat each other nicely. We all like to be treated nicely, don't we? Well, the Bible gives us an easy way to always remember how God wants us to treat others. It's called the "Golden Rule".

This rule is like a wonderful secret. It isn't really very hard. In fact, it's simple. Are you ready to learn God's special way to get along with everyone? *(Lean in and whisper.)* Here's the Golden Rule.

Treat others the way you want to be treated.
(Have the children wave their wrist bands and repeat.)

I'll say it again, just so we can remember.

Treat others the way you want to be treated.
(Have the children wave their wrist bands and repeat.)

Can you say it with me?
Treat others the way you want to be treated.
(Have the children wave their wrist bands and repeat.)

Good! Let's talk about that. How do you like to be treated? *(Allow children to answer; good, nice, and so forth.)* Those are good things. Now, how do you not like to be treated? What do you not like to have done to you? *(Allow children to answer; not liking it when friends are mean, being hit by someone, friends not sharing, and so forth.)*

I see. So, If someone hits you, and you don't like it, should you to hit back? No. Let's say the Golden Rule again.

Treat others the way you want to be treated.
(Have the children wave their wrist bands and repeat.)

If someone doesn't share with you, what should you do? Share with them, anyway. Then, they will learn from you the way God wants them to act. That's the Golden Rule!

Treat others the way you want to be treated.
(Have the children wave their wrist bands and repeat.)

If someone treats you badly, what should you do? *(Let the children respond.)* Be nice to them. Do you think they'll be surprised? Maybe next time, they won't be mean at all. That's the Golden Rule!

Treat others the way you want to be treated.
(Have the children wave their wrist bands and repeat.)

If you're in a new classroom and you want someone to talk to you, what should you do? *(Let the children respond.)* That's right! Talk to them. That's the Golden Rule!

Treat others the way you want to be treated.
(Have the children wave their wrist bands and repeat.)

Let's all say the Golden Rule together one more time.

Treat others the way you want to be treated.
(Have the children wave their wrist bands and repeat.)

In With BZ Bee

Bible Verse Buzz

hoose a child to hold the Bible open to Matthew 7:12.

Say: Today our Bible story is about an important rule Jesus taught his friends. We call the rule the Golden Rule. The rule tells us how God wants us to live.

Say the Bible verse, "Do for others what you want them to do for you" (Matthew 7:12, *Good News Bible*), for the children. Have the children say the Bible verse after you.

Turn your back to the children or hide your hands underneath a table or behind the **BibleZone™ FUNspirational™ Kit** lid as you place the **BZ Bee puppet** (see page 174) on your hand. Turn around or bring the puppet out where the children can see it.

Pretend to make the puppet talk. Change your voice for the puppet:

Bzzz. Bzzz. Bzzz. Hi, everybody! I'm BZ Bee. *Bzzz. Bzzz. Bzzz.* I like to taste fingers. Do you have fingers? Yum, yum, yum. Let me taste.

Go to each child. Encourage, but do not force, each child to hold up his or her fingers. Have BZ pretend to taste each child's fingers. Have BZ say things like:

Mmmm. Mmmm. You taste like honey.
Bzzz. Bzzz. You taste like strawberries.
Yumm. Yumm. You taste like blueberries.

After BZ has tasted each child's fingers, say:

Bzzz. Bzzz. Bzzz. I like to taste your fingers. They're yummy. *(Rub BZ's stomach.)*

Bzzz. Bzzz. Bzzz. I like something else even more than fingers.

I like the Bible. *Bzzz. Bzzz. Bzzz.* Today you heard a story Jesus told his friends. What did Jesus tell his friends about in today's story? *(a special rule, the Golden rule)* What did Jesus say to do? *(Treat others as you want them to treat you.)*

Bzzz. Bzzz. Bzzz. Jesus taught his friends an important rule. The rule tells us how God wants us to live.

 **We can treat others the way we want to be treated.**

Bzzz. Bzzz. Bzzz. Let's say the Bible verse together.

"Do for others what you want them to do for you" (Matthew 7:12, *Good News Bible*).

Have the children repeat the Bible verse with BZ Bee.

Have BZ Bee say good-bye to the children. Put the puppet away.

Bible

Choose one or more activities to immerse your children in the Bible story.

Supplies:
cassette player

Zillies™:
Cassette

Sing!

Say: Jesus taught his friends an important rule that we call the Golden Rule. The rule tells us how God wants us to live. This is the rule: "Do for others what you want them to do for you" (Matthew 7:12, *Good News Bible*).

Have the children repeat the Bible verse.

Say: That means if we want other people to be nice to us, we should be nice to them.

Play the song "Be Nice" from the **Cassette.** Have the children sing the words *be nice* each time they appear in the song.

Be Nice

When someone is mean to you
There's only one thing you should do,
this is my advice (What is it?)
Be nice. (Be nice?)
Be nice, be nice, be nice.

'Cause it's nice to be nice in all you do,
Not just when someone's nice to you.
If somebody calls you names,
Don't go out and do the same,
Remember this advice: (What is it?)
Be nice. (Be nice?)
Be nice, be nice, be nice, be nice, be nice.

When somebody bursts your bubble,
Better not start makin' trouble,
This is my advice: (What is it?)
Be nice.
Be nice, be nice, be nice, be nice.

Writers: Janet McMahan-Wilson and Debra Black
© 1991 New Spring Publishing, Inc. (ASCAP) (a div. of Brentwood-Benson Music Publishing, Inc.) All rights reserved. Used by permission.

From the Brentwood Music, Inc. recording *God's Way A Song A Day vol. 1*.

Choose one or more activities to bring the Bible to life.

Skip, Hop, Jump

Say: Jesus taught his friends an important rule that we call the Golden Rule. This is the rule: "Do for others what you want them to do for you" (Matthew 7:12, *Good News Bible*).

Have the children repeat the Bible verse.

Say: That means if we want other people to be a friend to us, we should be a friend to them.

Have the children stand in a circle in an open area of the room. Teach the children the song "I Want a Friend" to the tune of "Skip to My Lou." Sing the song several times. Then choose a child to begin the game. Have one child skip or gallop around the inside of the circle while everyone sings the song. On the last phrase, name a child in the circle. Have the skipper move to the child named, shake hands, and exchange places. The child named becomes the new skipper. Continue the game until each child has a turn moving around the circle. Vary the movement by substituting the words *hop*, *jump*, or *tiptoe* for the word *skip*.

I Want a Friend
I want a friend so what should I do?
I want a friend so what should I do?
I want a friend so what should I do?
I'll skip to my good friend *(name)*.

© Abindgon Press.

Supplies:
none

Zillies™:
none

Golden Grams

Photocopy the happy gram (**Reproducible 13B**) for each child. Write each child's name in the space provided with a gold or yellow crayon or marker.

Say: Jesus taught his friends an important rule that we call the Golden Rule. This is the rule: "Do for others what you want them do for you" (Matthew 7:12, *Good News Bible*). That means if we want other people to be kind to us, we should be kind to them.

Give each child her or his happy gram and **say:** *(Child's name)* is kind to others.

Let the children decorate their happy grams with crayons or markers.

Supplies:
Reproducible 13B, gold or yellow crayon or marker, crayons or markers

Zillies™:
none

Life Zone

Choose one or more activities to bring the Bible to life.

Supplies:
none

Zillies™:
none

Circle 'n Sing

Have the children stand in a circle. Sing the song printed below to the tune of "London Bridge." Repeat the Bible verse at the end of the song.

Jesus taught the Golden rule
(Walk around the circle.)
Golden rule, Golden rule
Jesus taught the Golden rule.
To teach us how to live.
(Stop walking.)

Supplies:
cassette player

Zillies™:
Cassette, "Smile! Jesus loves you" tote

Smile! Jesus loves...

Photocopy and cut apart the smile heart on page 116 **(Reproducible 9A)** for each child. Or use index cards. Write each child's name in large block letters on the hearts or cards. Place all the cards inside the **"Smile! Jesus loves you!" tote.** Have the children sit in a circle on the floor. Show the children the tote.

Say: Today we learned the Golden Rule that Jesus taught his friends.

 **We can treat others the way we want to be treated.**

Jesus was a special teacher. He taught us about God and God's love. We know that Jesus loves each one of us.

Pass the the tote around the circle. Play music from the **Cassette** or sing "Jesus loves me." Stop the music. Have the child holding the tote reach in and pull out a name card. Say the name printed on the card. Have that child stand up.

Say: *(Child's name),* **Jesus loves you. Thank you, God, for Jesus and for** *(child's name).* **Amen.**

Repeat the game until every name has been drawn from the tote and you have prayed for every child.

Photocopy the **HomeZone™** newsletter to send home to parents.

Home Zone For Parents

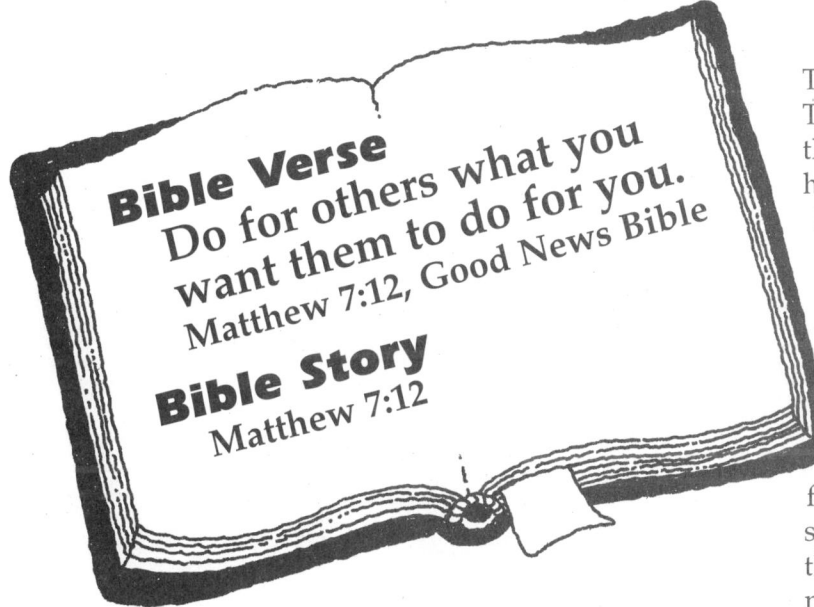

Bible Verse
Do for others what you want them to do for you.
Matthew 7:12, Good News Bible

Bible Story
Matthew 7:12

The Golden Rule

Today your child heard the Golden Rule. The rule summarizes the instructions that Jesus gives for holy living. It tells us how God wants us to live. The Golden Rule says to us that we should think about others and their happiness.

Young children may have difficulty applying the Golden Rule because they are unable to put themselves in another person's place. It is often difficult for them to view situations from anything other than their own perspective. However, they can understand that they like to be treated with kindness, and they need to be taught that others have these feelings too. Learning to respect the feelings of others is an important lesson of childhood, and indeed, of life.

Golden Goodies

Make this golden goodie treat with your child. Then practice the golden rule by sharing the goodies with friends.

different kinds of dry yellow cereal
fish-shaped crackers
yellow M & M candies.
resealable plastic bags
large paper bag

Purchase different kinds of dry yellow or gold cereal, crackers, and candies. Mix all the ingredients together in a large paper bag. Fold over the top of the paper bag and staple or tape the bag closed. Let your child shake the bag to mix the ingredients. Spoon the mixture into small resealable plastic bags and share.

We can treat others the way we want to be treated.

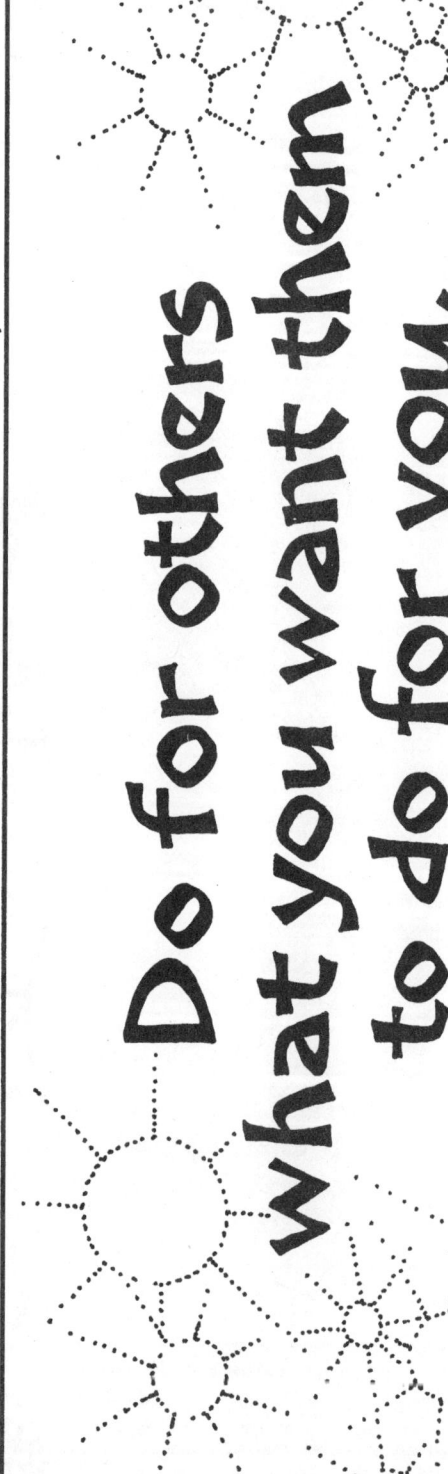

Do for others what you want them to do for you.

Matthew 7:12, *Good News Bible*

164

Reproducible 13A

Permission granted to photocopy for local church use. © 1998 Abingdon Press.

BibleZone™

Birthday Zone

Birthday Cheer

Use the suggestions in this Birthday Zone to celebrate birthdays. Have the children make a circle around the birthday child. Let the children walk in a circle around the child as you say:

> Hip, hip, hooray,
> It's *(child's name)*'s **special day.**
> Let's gather near
> And give a cheer.
> Hip, hip, hooray!

Have the children stop walking, jump up, and cheer for the child.

Birthday Jingle

Sing this song to the tune of "This Is the Way" to celebrate a child's birthday.

This is the way we light the candles,
Light the candles, light the candles.
This is the way we light the candles
On our birthday cake.

1, 2, 3, 4
(Count the number of candles for the child's age. Hold up a finger for each candle. Pretend to light the tip of each finger.)

Our friend *(child's name)* is four *(use correct age)* today,
Four today, four today.
Our friend *(child's name)* is four today,
Happy birthday, *(child's name).*

Birthday Buzz

Show the children the **BZ Bee puppet**. Pretend to fly the puppet around the room as you **say:**

> BZ Bee is buzzing
> All around the room.
> He's buzzing to the birthday girl *(boy).*
> Zoom, zoom, zoom.

Stop at the birthday child and have BZ Bee give the child a hug.

Game Zone

Christmas Memories

Supplies: nonbreakable Christmas items, tray, bandanna

Place several Christmas items on a tray. These might include a nonbreakable Christmas ornament, a bell, a Christmas card, a Nativity figure, a Christmas cookie cutter, and so forth.

Show the children the tray of Christmas items. Help the children identify each item. Cover the tray with the **bandanna** and have the children cover their eyes. Slip one of the items from under the bandanna and hide it behind you. Have the children open their eyes. Let the children guess what item is missing. When the children guess the item, put it back on the tray and play the game again.

Christmas Tree Pantomime

*Supplies: **Cassette**, cassette player*

Have the children move to an open area of the room.

Say: Let's pretend that we are decorations on a big Christmas tree. Let's be angels. When you hear me say "It's Christmas!" freeze right where you are.

Play music from the **Cassette**. Have the children pretend to be angels and fly around the room.

Stop the Cassette and **say: It's Christmas!**

Have the children freeze in an angel position.

Continue the activity, stopping the music each time and encouraging the children to freeze..

Movement suggestions:
  donkeys
  sheep
  popcorn (to string into a garland)
  Mary rocking baby Jesus
  a bell
  a bright star in the sky

Song Zone

Let the children listen to the song "The Bible Zone" from the **Cassette** as they enter the room or while working on lesson activities.

The Bible Zone

Where else can we find a lesson learned on every page?
Stories that have lived to teach us all from age to age.
From the flood to parting waters, burning bushes,
   prophets, scholars,
God's Word takes us anywhere.

In the Bible zone where God's Word comes to life.
In the Bible zone our path is always bright.
A book for all creation to every boy and girl.
In the Bible zone is God's treasure for the world.

In the Bible zone where God's Word comes to life.
In the Bible zone our path is always bright.
A book for all creation to every boy and girl.
In the Bible zone is God's treasure for the world.

Learning of forgiveness or when learning how to pray,
God's Word gives examples of the things we face each day.
When we choose to look inside, we see ahead or back in time.
God's Word takes us anywhere.

In the Bible zone where God's Word comes to life.
In the Bible zone our path is always bright.
A book for all creation to every boy and girl.
In the Bible zone is God's treasure for the world.

In the Bible zone where God's Word comes to life.
In the Bible zone our path is always bright.
A book for all creation to every boy and girl.
In the Bible zone is God's treasure for the world.

Words by David Hampton
© 1997 New Spring Publishing, Inc. (ASCAP)
(a div. of Brentwood-Benson Music, Inc.) All rights reserved. Used by permission.

Christmas Zone

Christmas Fun

Use the activities in this **ChristmasZone** when you need an extra or alternative activity. Remind your children that Christmas is Jesus' birthday.

Glitter Envelopes

Supplies needed: glitter; glue; shallow tray or box lid; glue brushes or cotton swabs; plain paper, crayons or old Christmas cards, paper punch, yarn

In Germany some people celebrate the birth of Jesus by writing letters to the Christ child. People sprinkle sugar on the letters to make them sparkle.

Give the children plain paper. Let the children decorate the paper with crayons. Have the children use glue brushes or cotton swabs to brush glue all over their papers. Place each paper in a shallow tray or box lid. Show the children how to sprinkle glitter over the glue. Shake off the excess glitter. Let the glue dry. Mail the letters to the children.

Or give each child the cover picture from an old Christmas card. Let the child brush glue over the card. Place the card in a shallow tray or box lid. Show each child how to sprinkle glitter over the glue. Shake off excess glitter. Use a paper punch to punch a hole in the top of each picture. Knot a loop of yarn through the hole to make a hanger. Hang the pictures around the room or on a Christmas tree.

Say: People all over the world are happy baby Jesus is born.

Christmas Zone

Bird Bangles

Supplies: toasted oats cereal in the shape of o's, green and red yarn

Give each child a length of red or green yarn. Wrap tape around one end of the yarn to make it easier to thread. Let the children string toasted oat cereal on the yarn. Tie the ends of the yarn together. Have the children hang the necklaces outside for the birds to eat.

Say: In two countries called Sweden and Norway, it is very cold at Christmas time and there is usually snow on the ground. On Christmas Eve some people place bundles of grain on poles outside in the snow for the birds to eat. Sharing food with the birds is one way some people celebrate Jesus' birthday. People all over the world are happy baby Jesus is born.

Play Dough

Supplies: play dough; glitter, ground cinnamon, or peppermint food flavoring

Add some Christmas fun to play dough.

Sprinkle glitter on a tray or shallow box lid. Give each child some play dough. Let the children take turns rolling their play dough into the glitter and working it into the dough.

Add Christmas smells by adding ground cinnamon or drops of peppermint food coloring to the play dough. Remind the children that the play dough is not safe to eat.

All About

_____
(Child's name)

Parent's Name_____

Address_____

_____Telephone Number_____

Child's Birthday_____Age_____

Child's Brothers and Sisters:

Name_____Age_____

Name_____Age_____

Name_____Age_____

Grandparents or other relatives your child sees often and is close to

_____

Nursery school, daycare, or other programs your child attends

_____

Allergies or situations in your child's life that the teacher should know

_____

Parents will be at

_____

BUZZ Into the BibleZone®

B U Z Z

Make Learning Bible Verses FUNspirational™ with BZ Bee.

Catch your children's interest with this delightful hand puppet.
It's soft!
Its mouth moves!

BZ Bee is two colors children love — hot pink and purple.

BZ Bee is part of every lesson for the first year of BibleZone™ (52 lessons).

It's durable!

Buzz to your local Christian bookstore and find me for $29.95. See you in the BibleZone™!

Abingdon Press

Comments From Users

Use the following scale to rate BibleZone™ resources.
If you did not use a section, write "Did not use" in the Comments space.

1 = In No Lessons   2 = In Some Lessons   3 = In Most Lessons   4 = In All Lessons

1. *Enter the Zone* provided information that helped me teach this lesson's Scripture.
   1   2   3   4   Comments:

2. The *Scope the Zone* chart made lesson planning easy.
   1   2   3   4   Comments:

3. The teaching plan was organized in a way that made it easy to use.
   1   2   3   4   Comments:

4. The Teacher's Guide provided easy-to-follow instructions for the learning activities.
   1   2   3   4   Comments:

5. The supplies necessary to do the activities were easily located in my home or church.
   1   2   3   4   Comments:

6. My students were able to understand the lesson's ZoneIn™.
   1   2   3   4   Comments:

7. The activities matched the learning level and abilities of my students.
   1   2   3   4   Comments:

8. The number of activities in the lesson plan worked for the time I had available (indicate how much time):_____.
   If not, check:_____ too many _____too few.
   1   2   3   4   Comments:

9. I used activities from the BirthdayZone section of the Teacher's Guide.
   1   2   3   4   Comments:

10. I used activities from the GameZone section of the Teacher's Guide.
    1   2   3   4   Comments:

11. I used activities from the ChristmasZone section of the Teacher's Guide.
    1   2   3   4   Comments:

12. I used the Cassette in my classroom.
    1   2   3   4   Comments:

13. I used items from the BibleZone™ FUNspirational™ Kit.
    1   2   3   4   Comments:

14. I sent the HomeZone™ page home to parents.
    1   2   3   4   Comments:

15. I used the BZ Bee puppet with my class.
    1   2   3   4   Comments:

ADDITIONAL COMMENTS

Activities my students enjoy the most are:

Activities my students enjoy the least are:

I use BibleZone™ for _____ Sunday School _____ Second-Hour Sunday School _____ Children's Church

_____ Wednesday nights _____ Sunday nights _____ Children's Fellowship _____ other

ABOUT MY CLASS

Number of children at each age in my class:

_____ Age 3 _____ Age 4 _____ Age 5

_____ Other (Specify) _____

Average number of children who attend my class each week: _____

I teach: _____ alone _____ with another teacher each week

_____ taking turns with other teachers _____ with an adult helper

ABOUT MY CHURCH

_____ Rural _____ Small Town _____ Downtown _____ Suburban

_____ Under 200 Members _____ 200-700 Members _____ Over 700 Members

Church Name and Address: _____

_____

My Name and Address: _____

_____

Please return this form to: Susan Salley
Research Department, UMPH
201 8th Ave., So.
P.O. Box 801
Nashville, TN 37202-0801